FIFTY PLACES TO HIKE

BEFORE YOU DIE

FIFTY PLACES TO

HIKE

BEFORE YOU DIE

**Outdoor Experts Share
the World's Greatest Destinations**

Chris Santella

FOREWORD BY BOB PEIXOTTO

STEWART, TABORI & CHANG

NEW YORK

This little book is for Deidre, Cassidy Rose, and Annabel Blossom,
and for everyone who's ever been inspired to set out on a new trail.

Contents

Acknowledgments 8 / Foreword 9 / Introduction 11

THE DESTINATIONS

ACKNOWLEDGMENTS

This book would not have been possible without the generous assistance of the expert outdoorspeople who shared their time and experiences to help bring these great hiking destinations to life. To these men and women, I offer the most heartfelt thanks. I want to acknowledge the efforts of my agent, Stephanie Kip Rostan, my editor, Jennifer Levesque, editorial assistant Wesley Royce, designer Anna Christian, and copyeditor Sylvia Karchmar, who helped bring the book into being. I certainly owe a debt of gratitude to the friends who introduced me, a suburban Connecticut kid, to the great outdoors, most notably Peter Marra. Lastly, I must thank my Mom and Dad for their constant encouragement, and the three ladies in my life—Deidre, Cassidy, and Annabel—for their generosity in time and spirit that allows me to spend so much time in the great outdoors.

FOREWORD

In our company mission statement, Leon Gorman, chairman of the L.L. Bean board and long-time company president, refers to the "physical and spiritual rewards that come from participation in outdoor activities." This spirit of health, personal renewal, and connection to the natural world is why I hike, and I imagine why so many of us do.

Hiking with my family has created irreplaceable memories for a lifetime, and has taught important lessons about keeping fit, and appreciating nature in both its majestic grandeur and in its smallest exquisite detail. While hiking I always want to learn more about the flora, fauna, geology, astronomy, meteorology, and cultural history of the area. We see, up close, nature's enduring qualities, and witness the changes brought on by our society's evolution. I would venture most of us concerned with conservation and environmental stewardship can trace our ethic to formative hiking experiences.

Hiking is a life sport that offers challenge by choice. Hiking can be a relatively easy, accessible, and contemplative activity with a short learning curve and not requiring expensive technical gear. At the other end of the spectrum we can select a hike that provides incredible physical challenges, that immerses us in wilderness solitude, or in the exhilaration that comes from taking risks to stretch oneself. Many of us study and acquire highly technical gear to enrich our experiences or, more honestly, for the sake of being first with the latest innovation. We can dabble in hiking, be fanatics, or anything in between.

In addition to being a physical, social, and educational experience, hiking is spiritual for many. There's nothing like ascending the shoulder of a mountain plateau to make one feel the presence of a higher power, up close and personal. Staring up at a starlit sky away from the lights of our modern world makes us feel infinitesimally small, and puts our petty endeavors and concerns into new perspective.

There's nothing quite like the intimacy of a friendship developed while hiking. Whether splashing along a trail in a driving rain, or traversing a spectacular ridgeline at sunset, shared experiences remove barriers, and we come to know each other through silly banter, deeply personal shared reflections, and through the intimacy of shared silences.

At L.L. Bean, we quip, "There's no such thing as bad weather, only bad equipment (or bad outerwear)!" I'm often struck by the fact that we plan our hikes around the weather; that we check and recheck the weather, and pray for ideal hiking conditions. Ironically, our most memorable experiences, those that we most frequently share with fellow hikers even years later, are the war stories that arise from being caught out in the least ideal conditions.

Finally, hiking is as much about the journey as the destination. We are a fraternity because we take the road less traveled by. Peak baggers can have a great time toiling all day to reach a tree-covered mountaintop with no view, just for the privilege of saying they've done it. Likewise, we think nothing of hiking eight or ten hours over rugged or barren terrain, to spend 15 minutes eating a cracker and some cheese on a remote summit in a howling wind.

Hikers have their favorite trails and favorite destinations. Like fishermen, hikers would prefer that some of their favorite hikes remain undiscovered and spared from heavy use. In *Fifty Places to Hike Before You Die*, Chris Santella shares his passion for great hikes, great trails, and great destinations. He has amassed a stellar list of the world's premier destinations; each with its own special ingredients that make them must do's. From Tibet to Tanzania, from Montana to Maine, Chris has prevailed upon a colorful cast of hiking enthusiasts to let the cat out of the bag and to share their favorite and most memorable hikes.

Enjoy the special stories and places on these pages. Use the book as an inspiration and a reference. Lace up your boots and add these destinations to your life list of future trailheads. Make your own memories, and see you on the trail!

—Bob Peixotto
  Chief Operations Officer, L.L. Bean, Inc.

INTRODUCTION

Long before the existence of bicycles, automobiles, skateboards, and even Segways, there were feet . . . and walking. While there are certainly faster ways to get from point A to point B, walking is still the best way to get a real sense of the surroundings you pass through—and still the only way to access some of the world's most remote locales, be they in the mountains of Bhutan or the deserts of Namibia.

I wrote *Fifty Places to Hike Before You Die* for those who value life in the slower lane, those who are inspired by the quest to get off the beaten track and immerse themselves in the diverse topographies of the natural world.

"What makes a destination a place you have to hike before you die?" you might ask. The chance to scale a mountaintop that most only view from afar? The opportunity to spy grizzly bears, ibex, and other charismatic species? The promise of close brushes with people in remote places whose cultures have changed little in recent centuries? The answer would be all of the above, and an abundance of other criteria. One thing I knew when I began this project: I was *not* the person to assemble this list. So I followed a recipe that served me well in my first six *Fifty Places* books—to see the advice of some professionals.

To write *Fifty Places to Hike Before You Die*, I interviewed a host of people closely connected with the walking world and asked them to share some of their favorite experiences. These experts range from National Park Service supervisors (like Sheridan Steele) to well-known mountaineers (like Jim Williams, Rob Hess, and Jim Sano) to leading wildlife biologists (like M. A. Sanjayan) to equipment manufacturers (like Phyllis Grove) to adventure-travel impresarios (like Nathaniel Waring). Some spoke of venues that are near and dear to their hearts, places where they've built their professional reputations; others spoke of places they've only visited once but that made a profound impression on them. People appreciate hiking for many different reasons, and this range of attractions is evidenced here. (To give a sense of the breadth of the interviewees' outdoors backgrounds, a bio of each individual is included after each essay.)

"Hiking" means different things to different people. For some, it may mean weeklong (or more) backpacking trips into the high country; for others, it may mean leisurely day walks with a late-afternoon return to a warm, dry abode. *Fifty Places to Hike Before You Die* attempts to capture the spectrum of these experiences, including a technical climb or two

and a few classic "inn-to-inn" walks geared for those less inclined to rough it. While this book collects fifty great hiking experiences, it by no means attempts to rank the places discussed or the quality of the experiences afforded there. Such ranking is, of course, largely subjective—the thrill of crossing Snow Lake, the largest ice field in Pakistan's Karakoram Mountains, may be anathema to someone who's more interested in a morning hike in the Texas desert! In this spirit, venues are listed alphabetically by state, province, or country.

In the hope that a few readers might embark on their own adventures, I have provided brief "If You Go" information at the end of each chapter, including the names of outfitters who offer guided hikes in the region at hand (if applicable). The "If You Go" information is by no means a comprehensive list, but should give would-be travelers a starting point for planning their trip. (Please note: Detailed information concerning specific trails— such as GPS coordinates, driving directions to trailheads, mileage between shelters, etc.—is not included here. The goal of this book is to offer a taste of the hiking experience at each place, not to provide a complete how-to guide. There's simply not enough room!)

One needn't travel to the ends of the earth to have a rewarding hiking experience. Yet a trip to a dream location can create memories for a lifetime. It's my hope that this little book will inspire you to embark on some new hiking adventures of your own.

OPPOSITE: A trek to the top of Mount Kilimanjaro holds a prominent place on many hikers "must do" lists.

NEXT PAGE: From the top of Grand Teton in western Wyoming, climbers can look out over Montana, Idaho, and Utah.

The Destinations

ARCTIC NATIONAL WILDLIFE REFUGE

RECOMMENDED BY **Eric Rorer**

"I can't recall exactly when I first had the urge to go to the Brooks Range in the Arctic National Wildlife Refuge [ANWR]," Eric Rorer began, "but I think it was when I was about thirteen. The description of this mountain range that was so wild and so remote stuck in my mind, even in junior high. Twenty or so years later, I was working for a dotcom in San Francisco. The company had an IPO that gave me a windfall of $7,000 in unexpected income. I had met a fellow who was a volunteer leader with Sierra Club Outings [part of the environmental nonprofit Sierra Club], and he described a trip he was going to be leading that summer in the Brooks Range. I signed up.

"The trip, in 1999, was to a place called the Franklin Mountains. Hiking through some of the valleys we visited, I had a distinct sense that these places had never been hiked through before. It was inspiring. That sense of remoteness is at the heart of the appeal ANWR and the Brooks Range have for me. When people ask why they should travel there when they could go hiking in the Sierras, or Wyoming or Montana or the other incredible places in the Lower Forty-eight, I say it's a chance to stand in a landscape that's truly wild. The Brooks Range is just like it was centuries ago . . . though climate change is beginning to have an impact."

If Alaska is America's last great wilderness outpost, then the Refuge is Alaska's most dramatic example of untrammeled nature. It comprises a South Carolina–size chunk of northeastern Alaska, abutting northwesternmost Yukon Territory to the east and the Beaufort Sea to the north, and bifurcated by the eastern edge of the Brooks Range. Of its more than nineteen million acres, approximately eight million are designated wilderness. The topography ranges from alpine (four of the tallest peaks in the Brooks Range are here) to tundra, creating a full range of arctic and subarctic ecosystems. Though at

OPPOSITE:

Backpackers
prepare breakfast
in the Phillip
Smith Mountains
of Alaska's Arctic
National Wildlife
Refuge.

17

times stark, this vast land reveals the richest variety of fauna in the circumpolar north, including all three species of North American bears, Alaska's largest caribou herd, and year-round resident musk oxen.

"After that first trip in 1999, I was asked if I might be interested in leading trips to ANWR," Eric continued. "I've led trips throughout the region every summer since then, from the far western part of the Brooks Range to just over the border of the Yukon Territory in the Richardson Mountains. We generally reach our point of departure via bush plane, though to control trip costs, I've also led trips that access the Brooks Range from the Dalton Highway. Trips generally go fourteen days; from my experience, it takes a solid week of being out there before you get into the rhythm of the landscape."

Hiking for days across glaciers and tundra with no other hikers for miles can give one a sense of tremendous solitude. Yet on occasion, that solitude can rapidly dissolve. "For several years, we hiked in the western section of the Brooks Range, hoping to catch a glimpse of the Western Arctic caribou herd," Eric recalled. "We missed them the first two years. The third year, we took a different route. Our hike started right on the coastline, headed straight south across the Arctic plain, and was slated to take us over the Brooks Range and along the southern slopes. On the third day of the trip, we reached the edge of a huge valley. Coming over the crest of a hill, we could see for miles in either direction— and there was a line of caribou extending as far as we could see." According to the Alaska Department of Fish and Game, the herd totals nearly 500,000 animals, and ranges over 140,000 square miles. Their travels from winter to summer feeding grounds have been likened to the great migration of the Serengeti.

For many, the totem animal of ANWR and its surrounding regions is the grizzly bear. Spotting one of these creatures is always thrilling and sometimes terrifying—especially if the animals display too much interest in you. "The most amazing bear sightings I've ever experienced were just outside the borders of the Refuge, in the Richardson Mountains of the northern Yukon," Eric described. "The Richardsons are extremely remote—even by northern Alaska standards—and the animals there seem as if they've never encountered people before. On this occasion, we hiked down into the end of a box canyon. At the bottom of the canyon, there was a major pile of caribou bones. It seemed as if some predator was herding caribou into the canyon and then preying on them. We worked our way farther along, had lunch, and then took a little nap. Our rest was interrupted when one of our participants stood up and said 'Oh s---!' Near the top of the canyon, a grizzly sow and two cubs were trying to chase down a baby caribou. The caribou managed to escape, but the sow kept coming down in our direction. We made noise to let her know we were there, and she shot up on her hind legs in a freaked-out sort of way. She seemed to look at us, then got back down on four legs and galloped around. She got up and sniffed the air again, then galloped toward us, making a huffing sound that grizzlies make when they're agitated. She came within twenty or thirty yards of us, just on the other side of a stream. She stopped, stared, took another few steps toward us, and then took off with her cubs. I'm still not sure if she was being aggressive or merely curious."

ERIC RORER is a professional photographer based in the San Francisco Bay Area. His photographs have appeared in *National Geographic Adventure*, *Sunset*, *California Home & Design*, *Newsweek Japan*, *Outside*, *Sierra*, *The Washington Post*, *The Los Angeles Times*, *The San Francisco Chronicle*, and numerous other publications. In addition to leading annual trips in the Brooks Range for Sierra Club Outings, Eric has hiked throughout the western United States and has a special weakness for the California desert. You may view some of his work at www.ericrorer.com.

If You Go

► **Getting There:** Most trips to ANWR will stage in Fairbanks, Alaska, which is primarily served by Alaska Airlines (800-252-7522; www.alaskaair.com). From here, your outfitter will arrange a charter flight into (or road transportation to the outskirts of) the Refuge.

► **Best Time to Visit:** The most reliable dates are from mid-June to late August.

► **Accommodations:** The Fairbanks Convention and Visitors Bureau (800-327-5774; www.explorefairbanks.com) lists lodging options in Fairbanks.

► **Guides/Outfitters:** Sierra Club Outings (415-977-5522; www.sierraclub.org/outings) organizes annual ANWR/Brooks Range adventures each summer. Trips are also led by Equinox Wilderness Expeditions (604-462-5246; www.equinoxexpeditions.com).

BANFF NATIONAL PARK

RECOMMENDED BY **Michael Vincent**

There are not too many places where you can enjoy world-class hiking in the morning and a five-star dinner in the evening. Banff National Park is one of them, thanks to 2,564 square miles of valleys, meadows, and mountains, and the presence of two first-class resort properties—Fairmont Chateau Lake Louise and Fairmont Banff Springs.

"I like to say that the Fairmont Chateau Lake Louise is a four-star resort in a five-star location," Michael Vincent began. "This is not a slight against the resort, but a testament to one of the most beautiful alpine settings in the world—there's a reason that the hotel sits where it does! You walk out of the hotel, and you're in the middle of a postcard, with forested hillsides sweeping down to the turquoise waters of the lake and Victoria Glacier gleaming in the distance. The vistas are tremendous from the Chateau and only improve when you get out on the trail."

Banff National Park comprises much of the southern border between the provinces of Alberta and British Columbia. That the Chateau and Banff Springs exist in the national park is thanks in large part to the Canadian Pacific Railway and the laws of supply and demand: The railroad created a supply of westbound train seats with the hope that some recreational centers would create a demand. The railway did not underestimate Banff's appeal. "The Banff Springs Hotel was built to appeal to the spa culture around the hot springs that bubbled up there," Michael continued, "and the original structure at Lake Louise—a log chalet with two bedrooms—was built for people interested in mountaineering. In 1899, several professional Swiss mountain guides were hired and brought to Lake Louise to help guests climb the surrounding mountains. The guides were let go in 1954, but in 1997 the notion of having staff guides was reincarnated. Today it's known as the Mountain Heritage Adventures program."

One would be hard-pressed to find a richer assortment of day hikes than those originating in the Bow River Valley of southern Banff; overall, the park has more than 900 miles of trails. From the Chateau, a half-mile of walking takes you into wild country; a few hours later, you're back in the comfort of an elegant lodge. According to Michael, the jewel of the extensive trail system around the lake is unquestionably the Plain of Six Glaciers hike. "The trail starts out along the lake, but climbs abruptly soon after," he said. "We gain 1,000 feet of elevation in the first mile, which is when we talk about grizzly-bear safety. The Lake Louise area has one of the highest densities of grizzlies in the park, despite all of the sightseers that come to gaze at the scenery. We don't see a bear on every hike, but it's not uncommon—in 2007, I had forty-two sightings.

"As the trail levels out, we start crossing avalanche paths. The avalanches clear out all the trees, and this leaves room for new vegetation to grow, which is essential for the pika (a relative of the rabbit), marmot, and other small animals that live here, and in turn, their predators, like the golden eagle. We soon come around a corner, and you walk into an IMAX film. Behind us is the lake and Chateau, ahead is the Victoria Glacier, thirty stories tall, and beyond that, Mount Aberdeen, Mount Lefroy, and the Mitre (a mountain shaped like a bishop's hat). Not far ahead, we come to the Plain of Six Glaciers Teahouse. This structure was initially built as a mountaineering hut by the Swiss guides, but now is run seasonally by a local family that serves tea and fresh-baked goods. While the teahouse is charming, I generally like to avoid the other hikers that might congregate here, so I like to push ahead to a little lunch spot among some boulders. Here we have our privacy and can take in the vista of all six glaciers: the hanging glaciers on Aberdeen, Lefroy, and Victoria; the Lefroy and lower Victoria valley glaciers; and the hanging glacier on Pope's Peak. This is also a great spot to view mountain goats, which frequent the talus slopes to the north. A few minutes farther along, you reach a lookout. You're tucked right under the glaciers of Mount Victoria, which reaches 5,000 feet above you; below you, there's a 200-foot drop, and shimmering Lake Louise in the distance."

There are innumerable hikes in the Bow River Valley of Banff, and Michael shared a few other favorites. "Helen Meadows is a trail that begins twenty minutes north of Lake Louise. Within the first hour of hiking, you're above tree line, with huge views of the valley the rest of the day. From mid-July to early August, the mountainsides are a carpet of color—wildflowers as far as you can see. Another astounding hike is the Larch Valley Trail. You climb 2,300 vertical feet; I almost call it 'hikeineering,' as there's some minor

climbing involved. If you do this walk in mid-September, the whole valley is gold, thanks to the larches."

With the long days afforded by a Canadian summer, there's plenty of time for nontrail activities. One must is a paddle on Lake Louise; the reflection of the lodge's red canoes mingling against the white of the glacier in the lake's trademark turquoise water is mesmerizing. "If visitors are interested in a libation, I always suggest the Lakeview Lounge," Michael added. "A big Palladian window looks out on Victoria Glacier. If you have a pair of binoculars, you can pinpoint exactly where you were earlier in the day."

MICHAEL VINCENT left his native Ontario in 1983 for the higher altitudes of the Rockies. He worked for Parks Canada for a decade, including as a National Park Interpreter. A passionate lover of the mountain landscape, Michael enjoys backpacking, skiing and snowboarding, rock and ice climbing, mountain biking, and whitewater kayaking. In 1997 he helped re-create the role of the Swiss Guides in the centennial ascent of Mt. Lefroy. He is an accredited member of both the Association of Canadian Mountain Guides and the Mountain Parks Heritage Interpretation Association. In 2002 he received the Award of Heritage Excellence from the Banff Heritage Tourism Corporation.

If You Go

▶ **Getting There:** Banff National Park begins approximately sixty miles west of Calgary, Alberta, and is served by many major carriers.

▶ **Best Time to Visit:** Mid-June through September offers the most reliable weather, and trails are generally free of snow at this time.

▶ **Accommodations:** The Fairmont Chateau Lake Louise (403-522-3511; www.fairmont.com) has 552 guest rooms. Other lodging options, including campgrounds, are outlined at the Banff Lake Louise Tourism website, www.banfflakelouise.com.

▶ **Guides/Outfitters:** Michael Vincent and his cohorts at Lake Louise Mountain Adventure Concierge (403-522-1601; cll.mountainadventureconcierge@fairmont.com) lead interpretive hikes.

OPPOSITE:
The Fairmont Chateau Lake Louise promises a bit of pampering at the conclusion of the Plain of the Six Glaciers trail.

SOUTHERN PATAGONIA

RECOMMENDED BY **Brady Binstadt**

Like Texas, Patagonia is as much a state of mind as a place. Encompassing roughly 400,000 square miles of vast steppes, groaning glaciers, spiky pink granite peaks, and electric-blue lakes, wind-pummeled Patagonia—divided between Chile and Argentina across the bottom of South America—is still very much a frontier. While it's relatively easy to disappear for weeks on end into one of the region's national parks, an expanding infrastructure of facilities for ecotourists seeking lodgings beyond a tent or hostel—and a few well-established estancias—make it equally plausible to set up a cushy base camp and do day hikes . . . or mix and match.

"You can't take a casual walk to Everest and check it out," Brady Binstadt offered, "but in southern Patagonia, you can walk to one of the most famous mountains on the continent and be back at your luxury hotel for dinner. Or you can do a multiday, ice cap traverse across a glacier. Or you can trek from one estancia to another. Beyond the unpredictability of the weather—it can be eighty degrees and sunny one day and thirty with snow the next—the hiking here is not very difficult. You don't have altitude considerations, as you're never hiking above three or four thousand feet, and elevation gains are rarely more than two thousand feet. Still, the sense of relief is much the same as in the Himalaya."

Though hard-pressed to name a single favorite, Brady offered a selection of hiking experiences that highlight this incomparable landscape. First on the list is a stay at Estancia Cristina, situated in an isolated valley on the shores of Lago Argentino, a surreal cobalt blue due to its glacial origins. Once a breeding sheep ranch, its 74,000 acres are now part of Glaciers National Park.

"As the crow flies, Estancia Cristina is just forty miles from the Fitz Roy massif," Brady continued, "but there's not another property for thirty miles. It's only accessible by boat

OPPOSITE:
Los Cuernos
del Paine is one
of Patagonia's
most iconic
mountain ranges.

or by walking in; if you boat in, you'll pass icebergs that have calved from Upsala, the continent's largest glacier. When a lot of walkers think of the area, they know Fitz Roy and Torres del Paine National Park. They may not know of the ranch, but once they stay there, it steals the show. You can go on a horseback ride and feel like you're out in wild Patagonia." There are a number of fine day hikes departing from Estancia Cristina, allowing visitors to take in glaciers, lakes, and ever-shifting mountain vistas. "For a more rigorous walk, you can trek north to another of the great estancias, Helsingfors," Brady added. "It's a five-day, four-night hike, and it's fully supported with guides, so you just carry a day pack." The path crosses seldom-traveled country, over the pass that divides the water-sheds between Lago Argentino and the region's other prominent lake, Lago Viedma. Helsingfors is right on Lago Viedma, and offers stunning views of Fitz Roy and the Viedma Glacier. A popular day hike from Helsingfors leads to the Blue Lagoon glacier. It's common to see condors and guanacos (a llama-like mammal) on this walk.

While the immense glaciers of Glaciers National Park may attract the lion's share of sightseers in southern Patagonia, most trekkers hope to spend some portion of their adventure approaching and gazing upon Monte Fitz Roy. The massif (its nonnative name honors the captain of Charles Darwin's expedition ship, the *Beagle*) is among the world's most iconic mountains, rising in jagged glory from the steppe. The town of El Chaltén rests just east of the mountain, and exists more or less to serve visiting hikers and climb-ers. "If you don't have the time or inclination to do a longer trek to Fitz Roy, there are three or four day hikes that are very accessible from downtown El Chaltén," Brady said. "One of the classic walks is to Laguna de los Tres. It's fairly challenging (fourteen miles round-trip with a vertical gain of 2,500 feet) and quite exposed at the end, but once you reach the laguna, you're looking up at 7,400 feet of vertical granite—more than two El Capitáns [the Yosemite rock face popular with climbers].

"You often hear about the wind in Patagonia," Brady added, "and I can attest to it. I was hiking near Fitz Roy on one occasion, and there was a steady thirty- or forty-mile-per-hour wind. A gust that must have been close to eighty miles per hour came up, and it literally blew me over. At the time, I weighed two hundred pounds and was carrying a full backpack. It was a reminder of what a powerful, wild place Patagonia is."

Many who travel to Patagonia hope to experience a taste of estancia life—a set piece of gauchos herding cattle or sheep in the shadow of snowcapped mountains, topped off by an *asado* complemented by local red wine. The culture of southern Chile was not as powerful an attraction for Brady as the outdoor opportunities, yet a lasting Patagonia memory concerns the hospitality of strangers. "I was toward the end of a three-day hike that concluded near an estancia. The weather had been very rough, and I was cold and tired from hiking for twelve hours. As I approached the estancia to say hello—I planned to continue on a few more miles into town—an older gentleman with a machete, wearing a little Patagonian hat (as if he were from a tourism pamphlet) walked out with a gourd of hot maté and a straw. He said, 'What's your hurry? Come in, stay for a while.' I went in, and there were seven other fellows working at the estancia. They had an *asado* going, and invited me to join them. I ended up staying for three or four days."

BRADY BINSTADT is the regional director for Geographic Expeditions, managing the travel company's programs in North and South America. He has traveled and worked throughout Europe and South America, including a yearlong stint teaching English in several Chilean towns. There he developed a love for the Spanish language and the history and cultures of Latin America. Brady graduated from Miami University (Ohio) with degrees in psychology and international economics.

If You Go

▶ **Getting There:** To visit Los Glaciares National Park and Monte Fitz Roy, fly into El Calafate, Argentina, which is served by LAN Airlines (866-435-9526; www.lan.com) and Aerolineas Argentinas (800-333-0276; www.aerolineas.com.ar) via Buenos Aires.

▶ **Best Time to Visit:** The austral spring and summer—October through March.

▶ **Accommodations:** Brady Binstadt recommends Estancia Cristina (+54 2902 491 133; www.estanciacristina.com), Estancia Helsingfors (+54 1143 151 222; www.helsingfors .com.ar), and in El Chaltén, El Puma (+54 2962 493 095; www.hosteriaelpuma.com.ar).

▶ **Guides/Outfitters:** The two estancias above have guides on staff. Fitz Roy Expediciones (+54 2293 436 424; www.fitzroyexpediciones.com.ar) leads day hikes and treks around Monte Fitz Roy. Geographic Expeditions (800-777-8183; www.geoex.com) orchestrates a variety of trekking-oriented adventures in the region.

GRAND CANYON NATIONAL PARK

RECOMMENDED BY **John Melville**

"Something that's very special about the Grand Canyon is that just about anyone can experience it," began John Melville. "Someone who spends an hour at the rim looking down has an inspiring experience—I haven't met anyone who has gotten to the rim and not said 'WOW!' Inspiring as the vistas are from the top, I must say that it's ten times as impressive if you see it from the inside out. The price of admission is physically demanding. But as you walk down, you see the history of the peoples of the canyon, and, perhaps even more fascinating, the history of the earth. You start on rocks put down 250 million years ago. By the bottom of the canyon, rocks date to 1.7 billion years ago—that's before there were continents. It's hard to get your head around it."

Neither the deepest nor the widest gorge in the world, the Grand Canyon is nonetheless recognized as one of the planet's most awe-inspiring erosion events—a 277-mile-long chasm that yawns from four to eighteen miles across and reaches depths of more than a mile, a seemingly endless series of abrupt cliffs and gentle slopes. The National Park Service reports that an average of 250 hikers are rescued from the Grand Canyon each year—usually because they didn't bring adequate water or take into account the intensity of the midday heat or the fact that at one point they'd have to hike back up to the rim. "Sometimes people forget that the Grand Canyon is really a desert," John continued. "When you're hiking out there, you realize how precious water is in these environs."

John has hiked and marveled at many of the trails in Grand Canyon National Park. When asked to isolate a few favorite hikes, two jumped to his mind: Trans-Canyon and Jewels of the Canyon. "The Trans-Canyon is certainly one of the park's classic hikes, the most recommended if you've never walked the canyon before," John explained. "It gives you a tremendous sense of accomplishment, as you actually cross the canyon. It also

OPPOSITE:
Backpackers
on Horseshoe
Mesa as they
descend into
the canyon via
Grandview Trail.

brings you to the North Rim, which sees only a fraction of the visitors that the South Rim experiences. The North Rim is 1,000 feet higher than the South, and as a result has Ponderosa pines and aspens. The colors are stunning in the fall. It's about fourteen miles from the rim down to the historic Phantom Ranch, and most people do it in a few days. The first day, you descend some 4,200 feet over seven miles. It's hard on the knees, but the views really help take the pain away. We camp at Bright Angel Creek that night, and follow the creek the next day down to Phantom Ranch. This day, we only lose 1,500 feet over seven miles.

"Phantom Ranch was set up as a tourist camp in 1900—Teddy Roosevelt and John Muir, among other notables, stayed there. They have a little canteen that serves the best lemonade in the world—at least, the setting makes it seem so! We usually have a layover day here, which allows time to explore secluded Phantom Canyon. It's a magical little world of waterfalls, pools, and little slides that you can glide down. The brilliant green foliage against the deep red and black rocks is visually stunning. While you're there, you should take a nocturnal adventure to the middle of a suspension bridge over the Colorado. The Grand Canyon is one of the most isolated (and hence darkest) places in the Lower Forty-eight, and the stars are absolutely brilliant.

"Most hikers will take the Bright Angel Trail from Phantom Ranch to the South Rim. The trail follows a geologic fault that was used by the Indians who once lived here. It's five miles to our next camp at Indian Gardens, where the Hualapai people once grew watermelons. One of my favorite parts of the hike comes on this afternoon. From our camp, we hike out to a spot called Plateau Point to make dinner. It's about 1,200 or 1,400 feet above Phantom Ranch. You're sitting out in the middle of the canyon, having dinner as the sun sets—and you only have to carry out your cookware.

"I'll never forget the finish of my first Trans-Canyon hike. As my group came out of the canyon, we were enveloped by a group of tourists visiting from Japan who'd just gotten off their tour bus. A few of us were asked where we'd come from, and we pointed across the canyon. We then explained in English, and the tour guide translated that we'd come from the other side. The whole group of visitors burst into applause simultaneously."

John's next trip departs from the South Rim. The Jewels of the Canyon hike takes its sobriquet from the mineral-named canyons you pass through—Turquoise, Ruby, Serpentine, etc. It covers portions of three trails—South Bass, Tonto, and Hermit. "This is not a hike that many people do," John continued. "Both South Bass and Hermit are considerably more challenging than the trails on the Trans-Canyon walk, and there's very little water or shade. In fact, you can only go in the winter and early spring, as by the end of April, there's no easily accessible water. None of these trails are officially maintained; it's not a place to go if you've never been before.

"One of the highlights along the Jewels of the Canyon walk is Boucher Canyon, before you reach Hermit Trail. From the Tonto Trail, you can follow Boucher Creek down to one of the most beautiful sand beaches on the Colorado. But you should think twice before jumping in for a swim—the river is just forty-five degrees, and drownings brought on by hypothermia are a major cause of death in the Grand Canyon." Another highlight in the early spring is the panoply of color availed by the native flora. "We often think of desert plants like cactus as being ornery and even ugly," John added. "But when cactus and prickly pear are blooming, they're wonderful.

JOHN MELVILLE is a volunteer trip leader for Sierra Club Outings, focusing on the Grand Canyon. When he's not leading Trans-Canyon hikes, he's an information technology manager at John Hopkins University in Baltimore, Maryland.

If You Go

▶ **Getting There:** For North Rim hikes, fly into Las Vegas (served by most major carriers) or Flagstaff, Arizona, served by several carriers, including Alaska Airlines (800-252-7522; www.alaskaair.com). For South Rim hikes, fly to Flagstaff or Phoenix.

▶ **Best Time to Visit:** Most hikers favor the early spring and early fall.

▶ **Accommodations:** For hikes departing from the North Rim, the nearest lodging is Grand Canyon Lodge–North Rim (877-386-4383; www.grandcanyonlodgenorth.com). For South Rim departures, Xanterra South Rim (888-297-2757; www.grandcanyonlodges.com) offers a number of options.

▶ **Guides/Outfitters:** There are many outfitters that lead hiking trips in the Grand Canyon, including Sierra Club Outings (415-977-5522; www.sierraclub.org/outings) and the Grand Canyon Field Institute (866-471-4435; www.grandcanyon.org/fieldinstitute).

THE OVERLAND TRACK

RECOMMENDED BY **James Fuss**

The Australian state of Tasmania rests some 150 miles south across the Bass Strait from Melbourne; it's sometimes called "the island off the island." "Tasmania has a unique landscape, even compared to mainland Australia," James Fuss began. "It's Australia, but not the Australia overseas visitors imagine from tour brochures. To put things in perspective, Tasmania is more than one-third larger than Switzerland. Although the highest peak just tops 5,000 feet, the island is considered the most mountainous island of its size in the world. Thirty-five percent of the island is protected by World Heritage and national-park status. The central part of Tasmania was once covered by a vast ice sheet, leaving some remarkable geology behind. It also boasts some of the best-preserved temperate forests left in the world. The coastline is stunning, with myriad coves, bays, beaches, estuaries, and spectacular cliffs. Tasmania is also a natural ark for many of Australia's unique mammals, birds, and alpine plants." (Those whose exposure to Tasmania has been limited to the Tasmanian Devil character from Warner Bros.' *Looney Tunes* cartoons may be surprised to learn that such an animal does exist; it's a carnivorous marsupial the size of a small dog that poses no danger to humans.)

A trek on the Overland Track is one of the best ways to experience the natural wonders of Tasmania. The roughly forty-mile walk, usually conducted over six days, takes you from Cradle Mountain to Lake St. Clair, through the heart of the Tasmanian Wilderness World Heritage Area, which encompasses some three and a half million acres on the west side of the island. "The Overland Track takes you across a landscape like no other in the world, with an unrivaled diversity that changes by the hour," James continued. "It has its challenges along the way, with several great side tracks, such as the scramble to the Cradle Mountain and Mount Ossa summits. The trail has many striking features—magnificent forests, wild alpine moors, pristine streams and waterfalls, all coupled with grand mountain scenery and a real sense of being in a truly untouched wilderness—a place that time forgot, which is wild and harsh and, at the same time, ecologically very fragile."

Most treks on the Overland Track begin in the north near Cradle Mountain; in the peak austral summer season, visitors are required to begin their trips in the north. Stopping places on the track are defined by the location of the five primary bushwalker's huts and camping areas. The huts are fairly bare-bones—rooms with sleeping platforms (no mattresses), communal cooking and dining areas, and composting toilets. You'll need to bring a stove and all of your food, and it's strongly advisable to bring a tent, in the event that there's no room at the hut. (The number of walkers on the Overland Track is closely regulated to help insure a quality experience, though hut occupancy is not.) A pleasant logistical aspect of the trail is that there are many side tracks convenient to the stopping points, allowing the more vigorous walkers in a group the chance to extend their day without wearying their cohorts.

Tasmania's endemic fauna is certainly an attraction for anyone embarking on a bushwalk here. Kangaroos themselves are not encountered on the Overland Track, but many other special animals are present. "Many of these creatures are nocturnal," James explained, "so they usually are encountered near camp around dusk and dawn. Wombats are common, especially near the start of the track, as are pademelons [a smaller relative of the kangaroo] and Bennett's wallaby. Potoroos [another kangaroo relative, also known as 'kangaroo rats'] are smaller again and more difficult to see. Tasmanian Devils are not common on the trail, but Tasmania's native cat, the quoll, is very active in the evening, hunting small prey. Without a doubt, my most prized sighting on the track was a platypus, which I came upon as it was feeding at the wombat pool on the first day of the walk." Platypus are perhaps the most enigmatic of Australia's roster of incredible creatures, a seeming fusion of otter (furry body) and duck (striking bill and webbed feet).

Craggy, imposing Cradle Mountain sets the tone for the trek to come. "I like to set out from Dove Lake and climb Cradle Mountain via Marion's Lookout, which rests above the lake," James said. "From the summit of Cradle, you can look south in the direction of the coming days' route. The view instills a sense of the true adventure that awaits." Waking to the songs of karrowong and yellow-throated wattle in moss-covered Waterfall Valley, day two takes you through sedgeland moors, past glacial tarns, and on to the shores of tea-shaded Lake Windermere. This walk highlights some of the Overland

Track's exquisite flora, including pandani (which resembles pandanus palms, but is a species endemic to Tasmania), eucalyptus, and pencil pines; some of the pines can live 1,000 years and more. Day three winds through gnarled forests below Mt. Pelion West before joining the Forth River, which leads you into the Lemonthyme Valley and onto the Pelion Plains. Between the lemonthyme, sassafras, and leatherwood that abounds here, this may be the most fragrant day on the track. The next day, you'll have an opportunity to conquer Mount Ossa, Tasmania's highest peak at 5,305 feet; from the summit on a clear day, it's said that you can see half of Tasmania . . . though one can't count on clear days in this part of the world. Beyond the Tasmanian Devil, one other aspect of the island that outsiders may have heard about is the weather. "It's certainly unlike anything else you've experienced in Australia," James added, "with one moment warm and sunny, the next windy and rainy, or even snowy."

The stretch of the Overland Track from Kia Ora hut to Windy Ridge brings you along the Mersey River and past three stunning waterfalls—Ferguson, D'Alton, and Hartnett. If you're thirsty, feel free to dip a cup into the river—the pristine streams of Cradle Mountain–Lake St Clair National Park are safe to drink from. For James, two highlights come on the last day of the hike. "As you enter Pine Valley, the landscape is striking," he effused. "The forests feel positively primeval—the only thing missing is the dinosaurs! Not long after, you reach the rock formations and wild peaks of Mt. Geryon, the Acropolis and the Parthenon. The way they're reflected in the glacial tarns that spread before them is truly unforgettable." Your adventure ends with a boat ride across Lake St. Clair to the town of Derwent, where the trappings of civilization await. "One of my fondest memories of the Overland Track is sitting by Lake St. Clair after completing the walk, with a bucket of freshly shucked oysters and a cold bottle of Pinot Gris, drinking in the privilege I've had to experience a wilderness wonderland on foot, being self-sufficient, taking only photographs, leaving only footprints, and killing nothing but time."

JAMES FUSS is a trekking guide, photographer, and chef extraordinaire. Born and bred in South Australia, James acquired his wanderlust early while exploring Australia extensively on camping trips with his parents. His love of the cooking arts began early as well, and after embarking on a career as a chef, he headed to Europe in the 1980s to extend his culinary repertoire. While there, he developed a real passion for the wilds of the British Isles and the Alps and spent four years traveling, backpacking, and cycling. He returned to Australia in 1990 to become a guide in the Outback. Since 1995, James has guided seasonally on three continents for Wilderness Travel. "It's a joy to be able to guide in such divergent places. I love the gastronomic diversity of Europe, especially France. In Nepal, it's not just the Himalaya but the genuine warmth of the people and the cultural wealth that bring me back. And I'm always happy to head back to Oz to help trip members discover my country's pristine wilderness, unique wildlife, bountiful seafood, and superb wines. Wherever I'm guiding, I try to make a journey a once-in-a-lifetime experience for people." James develops trips for Wilderness Travel in Australia and Europe and has conducted cooking seminars for the company's Nepal and Bhutan camp staff. When not guiding, James will usually be found at home in Tasmania, camping, boating, and fishing with family and friends, and "chucking a few shrimps on the barbie as well as fresh rock lobster and abalone." He is conversant in French, German, and Nepali.

If You Go

▶ **Getting There:** Most begin the Overland Track from the north, in Cradle Mountain–Lake St. Clair National Park. The nearest international airport is in Launceston, which is served from Sydney and Melbourne by Qantas (800-227-4500; www.qantas.com). There is bus service from Launceston via Tassielink (www.tigerline.com.au).

▶ **Best Time to Visit:** The austral summer (January through March) sees lower rainfall and warmer temperatures in Tasmania. From November through April, reservations are required; they can be made through Tasmania Parks and Wildlife Service (www.parks.tas .gov.au).

▶ **Accommodations:** Lodging options around Launceston are listed at www.discover tasmania.com. Options near Lake St. Clair at the conclusion of the trek are listed at www .lakesidestclair.com.au.

▶ **Guides/Outfitters:** A number of outfitters lead trips on the Overland Track, including Wilderness Travel (800-368-2794; www.wildernesstravel.com) and Cradle Mountain Huts (+61 3 6392 2211; www.cradlehuts.com.au).

LUNANA SNOWMAN TREK

RECOMMENDED BY **Steve Berry**

Lunana has been described as the most remote place in the most remote place, a valley closed off on all sides by high mountain passes in north-central Bhutan. Circumstances and coincidences seem to have been drawing Steve Berry in this direction for much of his life. "I was born just south of Bhutan, and my father was a Himalayan climber in World War II," he began. "I grew up with a solid expectation that I too would climb in the Himalaya. Through a series of coincidences, I got permission in 1986 to attempt an ascent of the highest mountain in Bhutan, Gangkhar Puensum (24,836 feet). The attempt was unsuccessful, but it further fueled my interest in the tiny Himalayan nation. In 1989 I was part of the second British party to enter the region of Lunana. The trail passes along the greener, southern side of the Himalayan chain just south of the Tibetan border, through uninhabited country up against the sides of unmapped peaks and through mountain passes up to 17,000 feet high. Most of the people of Lunana have never traveled beyond the mountains that surround the valley. It's fascinating to see the culture and the villages that have remained relatively unaffected by the outside world."

Most Westerners know little about Bhutan ("Land of the Thunder Dragon"), a tiny country the size of West Virginia that's sandwiched between India to the south and Tibet and China to the north. That's largely because until the last few decades, tourists were not permitted to visit Bhutan. This restriction was lifted in 1974, and today, a limited number of visitors are allowed, each paying a tariff of $200 a day. The tariff keeps out the backpacker types, who are less likely to contribute to the local economy. For their tariff, visitors get a visa, basic lodging, meals, and transportation. Visitors must also retain a certified guide for the entirety of their travels. Those fortunate enough to make the long journey are not disappointed. The Bhutanese are warm people, still very influenced by Buddhist traditions that seem mystical to the eyes of outsiders. In an effort to maintain its cultural heritage, Bhutanese citizens are required to wear traditional dress (at least on weekdays), kimono and bathrobe-type garments in brightly colored fabric that one often sees being woven on looms. Many residents live closely with their animals, and each spring they herd their yak high up into the mountains to spend the summer grazing on alpine pastures. Fortified monasteries guarding ancient temples (*dzongs*) cling to hillsides, defying gravity, while the towering mountains reach high into the clouds. Perhaps this proximity to the heavens helps lend Bhutan its sacred aura.

The Lunana Snowman trek is a massive undertaking, stretching nearly a month and 150 miles, often at altitudes exceeding 13,000 feet. The path begins near the city of Paro, heads north along the Tibetan border to the village of Laya, then east across the Karakachu La into Lunana and on to the trek's conclusion in the Bumthang Valley. The first few days of the trek move through heavily forested country along the Paro River. This region is frequented by Himalayan black bears, and trekkers are advised to hike in pairs, as the bears have been known to attack livestock and humans. You'll pass the base camp for mountaineers hoping to conquer Mt. Chomolhari (about 24,000 feet); dawn colors on the "Mountain of the Goddess" more than justify missing a few hours of sleep. As you continue toward Lunana, you'll sometimes come upon nomadic yak herders. Unused to encountering anyone on the trails—let alone westerners—the herders are likely to invite you into their yak-hair tents for a respite of yak-butter tea and curd from yak milk; most outsiders feel yak products to be an acquired taste! Entering the Lunana Valley, you're surrounded by pine-clad hillsides punctuated by thundering waterfalls. The valley floor is blanketed with heather, wildflowers, and brushwood.

You'll have a day to linger in Thanza, the largest village in Lunana, where you're likely to be feted. "Visitors are taken to meet the head man in the village, and a large party is organized. There's lots of singing, some dancing by the village women, and the *chaang* flows freely." [*Chaang*, which translates from Tibetan as 'nectar of the gods,' is a beerlike beverage generally brewed from rice, barley, or millet.] A few days later, you reach one of Steve's favorite points in the trek—the crossing of Gophu La, the trek's high point at about 17,200 feet. "It takes several days to go over the pass. The first day, we make it to the edge of the pass and camp at a lake that's surrounded by snowy peaks. The sunrise the next morning, as pink spreads down the glistening slopes and the whole scene is reflected back in the lake, is unforgettable. At the pass, dazzling Gangkhar

Puensum towers above the horizon. It seems to be a piece of earth that's been elevated to a higher, purer plane."

Hikers on the Lunana Snowman trek may encounter fascinating fauna in the high country. There are takin (Bhutan's national animal), a moose-size member of the deer family with an oddly shaped head that resembles a mix of musk ox and goat. There are also blue sheep, ibex, and wild yak. On a recent trek, hikers came upon a group of five snow leopards, one of the most elusive predators in the world. Steve Berry and his associates have made the Lunana Snowman trek some twenty times but have yet to encounter its namesake snowman, although the legend of the yeti runs deep in Himalayan culture. "Our guests speak of the yeti with a wink and a nod, yet our porters and the Bhutanese have detailed stories," Steve shared. "They say that there are two types of yeti: a small one that lives in the south and a larger specimen in the north. According to them, the yeti makes a sound that's like the whistle of a policeman, though it also has a tendency to mimic sounds. For example, if you were chopping wood, it might make a sound like chopping wood. Local people are not eager to see a yeti, as it's considered an omen of a nasty tragedy."

STEVE BERRY is managing director of Mountain Kingdoms, an adventure-travel company specializing in treks around the Himalaya and beyond. Born in Shillong, India, just south of the Bhutanese border, Steve has returned to the Himalaya many times as leader of numerous treks and expeditions, including the first British ascent of the Nun Kun massif in Kashmir, India, and attempts on Cho Oyu in Nepal and Gangkhar Puensum in Bhutan. His book, *The Thunder Dragon Kingdom*, is an account of Britain's first climbing expedition to Bhutan.

If You Go

▶ **Getting There:** This expedition generally stages in Kathmandu, Nepal, which can be reached via Hong Kong or Bangkok, Thailand. From Kathmandu, you'll fly to Paro, Bhutan, on Druk Air (www.drukair.com.bt).
▶ **Best Time to Visit:** The Lunana Snowman trek generally embarks in late September.
▶ **Guides/Outfitters:** Mountain Kingdoms (+44-1453-844-400; www.mountainkingdoms .com) leads the comprehensive trek described above.

OPPOSITE:
Solitude is easy to come by on the Lunana Snowman trek, which winds through some of Bhutan's most isolated stretches.

THE KALAHARI DESERT

RECOMMENDED BY **Ralph Bousfield**

If the average outdoorsperson—even the *very accomplished* outdoorsperson—were stranded in Botswana's Kalahari Desert, he or she would almost certainly perish, unless taken into the care of the Zu/'hoasi Bushmen.

"The Zu/'hoasi have called this region home for at least 35,000 years—some archeologists believe it's closer to 70,000 years," began Ralph Bousfield. "Their occupation of these lands comprises the longest continuous human habitation of any place on earth. The habitat here is unrelentingly harsh—it's one of the driest places on earth. Yet the Zu/'hoasi have such an understanding of their homeland, they're able to find enough moisture to survive. There's also a powerful ethos of cooperation in the culture. It's a survival tactic; they understand that if you go it alone and don't share, you die. A walk with the Zu/'hoasi is not a walk solely for the beauty of the landscape, or an opportunity to see the many animals that call this area home. It's a walk through time and through a culture."

The Bushmen that Ralph Bousfield has known since his youth live around the Makgadikgadi Pans, more than 6,500 square miles of salt flats, grasslands, and sand dunes that are remnants of an immense salt lake. To some eyes, it may seem bleak and featureless, but for the Zu/'hoasi, each inch is animated. "Every rock, every bush, has a name and a story, it seems," Ralph continued, "and these stories come out on our walks." Ralph leads several such walks with the Bushmen, offering visitors a chance to visit their camps, sample their fare (including wild spinach and ostrich-egg omelets), gather medicinal plants, or even hunt small animals, such as porcupines. But the ultimate opportunity to immerse oneself in the ways of the Zu/'hoasi is to accompany a Bushmen initiation hunt, both a rite of passage for tribal men and an important food-gathering event.

There are no established circuits that you walk when you join a hunt. "Where you walk on a given day is decided by the old shamans in the tribe," Ralph explained. "They take out these wood divining disks that they use to talk to ancestors. The ancestors tell them where to go to find eland [African antelope]. It sometimes transpires that the disks say, 'Don't go out today.' However, the ancestors tend to be helpful spirits. If the disks say, 'Don't go out,' the shaman may throw them down again and get a different response.

"When we do set out, we'll walk on old elephant trails. The walk is very relaxed, even chatty. The Zu/'hoasi are a very social society. As you walk along, someone may point out a bush and say that it has its leaves early this year. Someone else, looking at the bush, may point out beetle droppings, and this will lead another person to try to dig up beetle grubs so poison can be extracted for use on the tips of hunters' arrows. Then a few of the other Zu/'hoasi will gather up some sticks and make a fire, and a pipe of strong tobacco will be stoked up and passed around. As an outsider, you're left thinking, 'We'll never come across an animal this way!' But when the Bushmen pick up animal tracks that are less than a half-hour old, it's all business. There's absolute silence; the men communicate in sign language. After analyzing the tracks, individual hunters will start taking on the mannerisms of the animal they're tracking. They'll mimic the animal's stride—this will help them gauge the creature's size and its needs. They understand the nuances of every movement. For them, interpreting the tracks is like reading the newspaper—it gives them an up-to-date perspective of their world."

The eland—the largest member of the antelope family—is the most prized target for the Zu/'hoasi. This is because of the great amounts of fat these animals carry. "In Western cultures, fat has almost become a taboo," Ralph continued. "In the Kalahari, the fat of the eland is invaluable as it's a foodstuff that can be stored."

The Zu/'hoasi are able to get very close to the eland; the animals don't associate people with hunting, as there are no guns. Instead, the Bushmen use tiny bows with a modest thirty-pound pull. Their arrows, however, are tipped with a powerful poison (from the aforementioned beetle grubs). "The arrow tip is the size of four matchstick heads," Ralph explained. "When the eland is hit, it doesn't realize anything has happened; it's as if it were stung by a bee. The hunters will know exactly how good the hit is by the color of the blood, and they'll have a good sense of how long the poison will take to have its effect. Once the tracking begins, the Bushmen's incredible sensitivity to their environment is apparent. After the eland has fallen and been dispensed with a spear, the meat is distributed according to a complex set of tribal rules. For the young men participating in the hunt, it's the ultimate moment in their lives. Within days of the hunt, word will have traveled to other tribal members 100 or 200 miles away.

"Humans have been on Earth for somewhere between two-and-a-half to four million years," Ralph added. "Until 10,000 years ago, every single person was a hunter-gatherer. When you see the Bushmen on a hunt or gathering plants or honey, you realize they're doing exactly what we as a species were preordained to do. Initially, guests react by thinking, 'These folks are so different.' But after a few days around the Zu/'hoasi, they begin to identify with individual tribal members. They see that the Bushmen share many of the same worries and insecurities. Pretty soon, we're just friends sitting around a fire."

RALPH BOUSFIELD comes from a long line of African pioneers and adventurers; his family has guided safaris for five generations. Ralph studied Nature Conservation and did his thesis on the Wattled Crane as an Indicator Species of Wetland Destruction. He furthered his studies at the International Crane Institute in Wisconsin under the famous George Archibald, who captive-bred the whooping crane back from extinction. Ralph then worked with his mother to establish Botswana's first Wildlife Orphanage and Education Centre. In 1998, Ralph co-produced and presented a sixteen-part series for the Discovery Channel entitled "Uncharted Africa," which was filmed in Botswana, Namibia, Kenya, and Tanzania. He established Uncharted Africa in 1993 with Catherine Raphaely, in memory of his legendary father, hunter and safari operator Jack Bousfield.

If You Go

▶ **Getting There:** To reach Jack Bousfield's Kalahari camps, travel to Maun, Botswana, which is served by Air Botswana (800-518-7781; www.airbotswana.com) from Johannesburg. From Maun, a charter flight takes you near the current camp's location.

▶ **Best Time to Visit:** The Bushmen initiation hunt is generally conducted in late April. Other walks are conducted throughout the year.

▶ **Guides/Outfitters:** A number of Bushmen walks are offered by Uncharted Africa (+27-11-447-1605; www.unchartedafrica.com) and are made possible by Jack Bousfield's long relationship with the Zu/'hoasi.

THE LOST COAST

RECOMMENDED BY **Seth Levy**

One of the perks of working for an organization like the American Hiking Society (AHS) is that your job requires a certain amount of field research. Such "work" demands brought Seth Levy to the King Range Conservation Area, known to some broadly as the Lost Coast. "I was working on a project to protect some of the Bureau of Land Management's (BLM) most spectacular landscapes—called the National Landscape Conservation System. As I was reviewing background materials, the Lost Coast caught my attention. AHS coordinates an annual trail-maintenance trip there as part of our Volunteer Vacations program. Leading this trip seemed like a great chance to meet some of the land managers at the King Range, do some trail work, and see some of the West Coast."

The King Range National Conservation Area is a splendid meeting of land and sea, stretching thirty-five miles along the Humboldt County coast, from the Sinkyone Wilderness in the south to the Mattole River in the north. While much of California's coastline has seen development of varying levels, this region was deemed too hardy for highway construction; with Highway 101 pointed inland, a swath of land amounting to 68,000 acres has been preserved, largely in its native state. The conservation area is land of great contrasts—mountains rise precipitously from black-sand beaches; King Peak, the highest point in the area, stands at 4,088 feet, just a few miles from the Pacific. In between are ancient forests of Douglas fir, golden prairies seasonally festooned with wildflowers, and fern-shaded creeks that trickle modestly in the summer months and surge violently with the hard winter rains.

There are eighty miles of trails within the King Range National Conservation Area. Some, like the King Crest Trail, straddle the preserve's rugged coastal ridge; others, like the Saddle Mountain-Rattlesnake Ridge-Buck Creek Loop, offer a mix of mountains and

sea. If there's one hike that defines the region, however, it's the twenty-four-mile north leg of the Lost Coast Trail—one of America's few coastal wilderness hikes. When asked what makes the Lost Coast Trail special, Seth's answer was succinct: "It's beach. Almost all trails are terrestrial, but this is half terrestrial, half aquatic. On some hikes, you may occasionally smell the sea breeze if the wind is right. On this trail, it's immediately present. In fact, there may be times when you're walking with one foot in the water and one on land. It's essential to have a tide table when you're out there, and you need to know how to read it. There are parts of the trail that are underwater at high tide, and if you're not careful, you could find yourself in a tough spot."

A walk on the Lost Coast Trail does not unfold completely at sea level. The trail climbs up onto ledges and along cliffs above the beach, and traverses broad wildflower-covered slopes before returning to the water. Still, the Pacific is the star. "There's a fantastic ocean-front view for much of the hike," Seth continued. "It can't be helped. It's not just watching soaring gulls overhead, but observing seals, sea lions, orcas, and dolphins out beyond the surf. The view of Sea Lion Rock is spectacular—as the name suggests, it was just covered with pinnipeds." Flippered mammals are not your only companions on the Lost Coast. Black bears will frequently cruise the beach, especially in drought years, looking for morsels. "They've been dubbed 'beach-bum bears,'" Seth added, "as some in the past have shown a proclivity to pursue the easy meal of campers' food. To protect the bears, backcountry hikers are required to take bear canisters for food storage." The streams along this coast have helped create safe and inviting campsites. "In most places, it's not safe to sleep on the beach, as you could find yourself stuck between a sheer cliff and the ocean," Seth said. "But there are coves at five-to-ten-mile intervals where a river has eroded a section of beach. The result is a broad, grassy expanse set back from the ocean, cut through by a clear stream, which provides your water. These natural campsites are ringed with pine trees, and you have the mountains behind you and the ocean in front of you."

For Seth, hiking the Lost Coast as part of a Volunteer Vacation only enhanced the overall experience. "Doing the trail is great, but mixing your hiking with stewardship makes it a much richer adventure. The ability to look back at a trail and not simply say, 'I did that,' but, 'I made that,' is incredible. In many cases, you'll also receive some special attention from the land managers, who are generally eager to show appreciation for your efforts." If you happen to be working on the Lost Coast Trail, that special attention takes the shape of a celebratory evening above Shelter Cove. "The BLM has access to a gorgeous

OPPOSITE:
The Lost Coast Trail's beachside location allows for atypical off-trail activities.

cabin that sits on a bluff that overlooks much of the Lost Coast," Seth recalled. "The cabin is closed to the public, but they opened it up for us. At the hike's conclusion, they brought the whole group up for a salmon dinner. And instead of setting up our tents for the night, we got to stay in comfortable rooms. I still think about watching the sun set into the Pacific, feeling the warmth fade from the air, and then watching the moon rise up over the towering King Range behind us."

SETH LEVY joined the American Hiking Society in 2005 to protect trails on Bureau of Land Management lands, and managed the organization's Western Public Lands Initiative. He graduated from the College of Wooster with a BA in philosophy, concentrating in environmental law. His employment history includes experience in the federal government, conservation organizations, and outdoor retail. Seth has completed the Long Trail and more than half of the Appalachian Trail. As of this writing, he has left AHS to continue the AT.

If You Go

▶ **Getting There:** The closest commercial airport is in Arcata, California served by United (800-864-8331; www.united.com) and Alaska Airlines (800-252-7522; www.alaskaair.com).

▶ **Best Time to Visit:** The King Range Conservation Area is open year-round, though conditions are best from late spring through early fall. The Bureau of Land Management provides in-depth information about hiking and camping opportunities in the area at www.blm.gov/ca/st/en/fo/arcata/kingrange/index.html.

▶ **Guides/Outfitters:** The American Hiking Society (www.americanhiking.org) offers annual volunteer vacations to the Lost Coast.

YOSEMITE NATIONAL PARK

RECOMMENDED BY **Kari Cobb**

If you were to herd a group of national-park employees, passionate day hikers, and back-country enthusiasts into a room and pose the question, "What is the jewel of America's national park system?" voices would rise, fleece would fly . . . and odds are good that Yosemite would hold its own in the straw polls. Yosemite has the "wow!" factor of its famed valley, which attracts the lion's share of the more than three million people who visit the park each year. Many don't realize that a vast majority of the park's nearly 1,200 square miles is maintained as wilderness terrain, flowing across a swath of the western flank of the Sierra Nevada—the mountains that John Muir called "the range of light." More than 750 miles of trails run through the wilderness area, with another fifty or so in the valley.

Perhaps no national park is so closely associated with one individual as Yosemite is connected with Muir, a Scotsman who emigrated to the United States in 1849 at age eleven. He spent his formative years working on his family's farm in Wisconsin, where he also found time to create inspired inventions from wood, including a contraption that would flip him out of bed before dawn. After a stint in college and several years wandering the Midwest and Canada supporting himself with odd jobs, Muir suffered an injury while working in a carriage-parts shop in Indianapolis in 1867, resulting in temporary blindness in one eye. This was an epiphany; when his sight returned, he vowed to use the gift of vision to take in nature's wonders. He made his way to Florida and then California, and soon after discovered the Sierra Nevada and the land that would become known as Yosemite. Though he eventually would call the Bay Area home, his heart belonged to the Sierra high country, which he captured in his most influential writings. His articles chronicling the ravages of sheep and cattle grazing in the high country helped lead to the creation of Yosemite National Park. He went on to help establish and champion many of

47

the principles that would guide America's parks system, and along the way founded the Sierra Club to "do something for wildness and make the mountains glad."

Of Yosemite's many iconic images—its waterfalls, its giant sequoias, the rock climbers scaling El Capitán—Half Dome perhaps looms largest in our collective consciousness. This granite monolith is visible throughout much of Yosemite Valley, rising 4,800 vertiginous feet above the valley floor to an elevation of 8,800 feet. Once thought unassailable, today it is summited by countless hikers—on busy summer weekends, as many as 1,000 in a day—thanks to steel cables that were affixed on the final 400 feet of the ascent in 1919. Even without its cable-enabled finale, Half Dome is a rigorous test—a fourteen-plus-mile round trip from the valley floor, with nearly a mile of elevation gain. Few would deny those who tackle the climb a bit of gloating as they recline on Half Dome's level top.

"It's no surprise that many people who visit Yosemite want to hike Half Dome," Kari Cobb said. "When I began working at Yosemite, it was one of the first things I wanted to do. It's a great hike, but not my favorite. I cherish Yosemite for the solitude it has to offer. I treasure every moment I'm in the backcountry and don't see anyone else, and only have to think about the birds flying by, and water dripping off the mountainsides.

"I've worked in the Tuolumne Meadows and Tioga Pass areas of the park, and most of my favorite backcountry hikes are there. The first leads up to the Vogelsang High Sierra Camp. It's a strenuous hike—almost fourteen miles round-trip. It begins calmly on the John Muir Trail, making its way through Lyell Canyon along the Lyell Fork of the Tuolumne River. [The famous John Muir Trail begins in Yosemite Valley and runs south some 215 miles, ending on Mount Whitney, the tallest mountain in the Lower Forty-eight.] At Rafferty Creek, the trail splits off and gets steep quickly. Many people turn around here. If you continue, you get some solitude and eventually reach Tuolumne Pass. I like to make it an overnight trip and continue a few miles past Vogelsang to Gallison Lake—one of the most beautiful lakes I've ever seen. Gallison sits peacefully down in a little valley, and there's never anyone there. The first time I ventured there, I stared down at the lake for over half an hour. My friends finally said, 'Okay, enough pictures!' Coming around the corner and seeing Gallison Lake tops everything I've encountered in the park—or anywhere, for that matter!

"Another hike I like very much is over near Tioga Pass, to Mount Dana and onward to a place called Kuna Crest. The first part is on trail, the second off. Most visitors don't

OPPOSITE:
A majority of
Yosemite's three
million visitors
don't wander
beyond the
valley, even
though the
park offers an
abundance of
backcountry
opportunities.

realize that Yosemite has no policy that requires people to stay on the trails; the only restriction on off-trail hiking is for large groups. There are so many places in the park that people don't experience because they don't want to go off trail." Mount Dana, at 13,060 feet, is the second-highest peak in Yosemite, and reaching the summit requires no technical skills, only sturdy lungs. "You can reach the summit of Mount Dana in a few hours, as it's less than four miles," Kari continued. "As you'd expect, the views are amazing, and include Mono Lake. I especially like the colors up there at sunset. From Mount Dana, I like to extend my hike over to Kuna Crest. As there's no trail, you need a good map . . . and having someone along who's familiar with the route doesn't hurt, either. I bring along National Geographic Map 206—they send their maps to us before they're published so we can review and correct any errors. En route to Kuna Crest, there are small lakes that remain frozen all year. They have a spectacular turquoise color."

KARI COBB has been a park ranger in Yosemite National Park since 2004. She graduated from the University of California at Santa Cruz in 2007 with a BA in sociology and a minor in legal studies. She furthered her education at Fresno State in Fresno, California, by obtaining an MS in criminology in 2009. When she's not at work, you will find her hiking in the Yosemite backcountry looking for the next secret spot of solitude.

If You Go

▶ **Getting There:** The Fresno–Yosemite International Airport is served by many airlines, including Alaska Air (800-252-7522; www.alaskaair.com) and American (800-433-7300; www.aa.com). Yosemite is approximately four hours' drive from Bay Area airports.

▶ **Best Time to Visit:** Yosemite is open year-round, though snow often covers the high country from November until late May.

▶ **Accommodations:** In addition to the campsites provided by the Park Service, Yosemite National Park Vacation and Lodging (801-559-4884; www.yosemitepark.com) offers more comfortable accommodations ranging from basic tent-cabins to the luxurious Ahwahnee hotel.

THE THREE GORGES

RECOMMENDED BY **Jim Williams**

"I have a background in developing and leading remote trips of an exploratory nature," Jim Williams began. "And that was what initially led me to the Yangtze River, almost thirty years ago. The great history of China, especially the Three Gorges area, held a mystique for me. I've always had a curiosity about topics that you couldn't learn much about. When I was in school, we didn't learn much of anything about China, beside the fact that Chinese people had slanted eyes, invented gunpowder, and lived on the other side of the earth. On that first excursion, the tour group I was with—a company known for its luxurious trips—motored upriver on an opulent river cruiser. It was the classic 'Introduction to China' trip available at that time. As we cruised along, my father kept saying, 'There has to be another way up river. People didn't just take boats.' At one point, I looked up and saw these paths carved into the vertical limestone cliffs lining the river—paths that were once used by people called *trackers* to tow boats upstream for hundreds of years before the age of motorized travel.

"I came back to the Yangtze a few years later and began to research the possibility of a different way of exploring the Three Gorges area. I hired a small, shallow-draft boat with an engine that was strong enough to go against the current and pull up to the shore, so we could get out and walk along the towpaths. It was not a trek per se, but an exploration that involved a good deal of hiking, both along the river and into side canyons along the way."

Beginning high in the Tibetan Himalaya, the Yangtze is China's longest river, flowing almost 4,000 miles to the East China Sea. As the Mississippi River divides the eastern United States from the west (at least on a psychological level), the Yangtze separates the north and south of China—and has provided a commercial artery for millennia. "Historically speaking, going beyond the Yangtze was a milestone," Jim continued. "For

Chinese people on either side, crossing the river was like going off to the frontier." Between the cities of Fengjie and Yichang in the Hubei province rests the hundred-odd miles of the Three Gorges, one of the river's most storied sections—and certainly a region that's gained a level of notoriety since the construction of the Three Gorges Dam. "Here, roiling waters take hairpin turns between sheer limestone mountains," Jim described. "By getting out of the boat and hiking along the river, visitors can get a feeling for life along the river, and can imagine what it was like to live here hundreds of years ago. It allows us to get off the tour-boat circuit and interact with residents on a much more local level." After a moment, Jim added that time is short to hike the towpaths of the Three Gorges. "Much of the Three Gorges will soon vanish beneath the waters of the dam [China's most massive engineering project since the Great Wall]. It will ultimately create a 370-mile-long reservoir that will inundate 1,400 villages, entire large cities, and some of China's most fertile agricultural land, forcing nearly two million Chinese from their ancestral homes."

The trackers who worked the Yangtze led difficult and often dangerous lives. Crews of forty or fifty men were harnessed to bamboo cables hundreds of yards long, which, in turn, were connected to barges and other craft bearing goods. The tracker crews labored along narrow towpaths, often struggling to pull their burden through treacherous rapids far below; one misstep could prove deadly. Life in the gorges of the Yangtze is eloquently captured in the following passage from John Hersey's 1956 novel, *A Single Pebble*, which is told from the point of view of an American engineer sent to the great river to evaluate potential dam sites:

The limestone formations fell away, and we moved all at once into a region of plutonic rocks. In a valley, nearly a mile wide, huge boulders of gneiss and granite, larger by far than our junk, lay strewn about, and straight across the line of the river, relenting only enough to grant it a shallow channel, curious dykes of greenstone and porphyry rose up out of the other stone. It was a primeval landscape, and it seemed to have been arranged by some force of fury. I was deeply moved and humbled by the sight of the trackers scrambling like tiny, purposeful crickets over the rough and intractable banks. We were all hopeless insects in this setting.

OPPOSITE:
A walk along the Three Gorges section of the Yangtze illuminates a bit of old China, although change is coming rapidly.

Moving upstream, the first gorge you'll come upon is Xiling, and here you'll take your first towpath hike. "This path leads to the small trading town of Peishi, which has intact

Ming-style buildings, with post-and-beam construction and upturned tile roofs," Jim described. "The next day, we hike the paths of the Wuxia (Witches' Gorge), a fantastic, narrow canyon lined by twelve jagged, cloud-piercing peaks soaring to 3,000 feet. Before reaching the last and most spectacular gorge—Qutang—we detour to the Daning River and walk the cliff paths of the Dragon Gate Gorge, some of which date to the third century BC, and visit the Ming-dynasty village of Dacheng. Making our way upriver, we pass terraced fields of potatoes and wheat, dense thickets of bamboo (and vendors selling all things bamboo, from baskets to shoes), and get to view the bustle of the river (which carries three quarters of China's river commerce), from long barges to small sampans and tourist boats that might carry 700 passengers.

"I've been traveling the Yangtze for almost thirty years, and things have certainly changed with the construction of the dam. Yet at the same time, things are going on much as they were in the olden days. When you go into a settlement, it's difficult to tell the old elements from the new. Things age quickly in China."

Food memories linger long, and culinary encounters often offer startling insight into the distinguishing characteristics of a place. Jim recalled one such Yangtze memory with a song. "On one of my earlier exploratory trips up the Yangtze, we pulled into a small town, tying up our boat along its floating docks. It was late in the evening and there were few dining options available, but we eventually found a spot where there was a collection of enormous clay pots—four feet tall, two feet wide—and a few tables. We didn't know what was being cooked and couldn't understand the dialect of our server, but we were hungry and sat down for dinner. The first course was crawfish—there's now a huge commercial crawfish industry along the river. Then the second course came, big pots filled with items we couldn't identify at first. Upon closer inspection, we determined they were pig parts—snouts, intestine, hooves. My younger sister, who's quite musical, was with us. She started singing the tune of the sixties ballad 'Where have all the flowers gone?' but changed the words to 'Where have all the pig parts gone?'"

JIM WILLIAMS founded Exploradus in 1985, an exploration-travel company dedicated to exploring remote areas of the world, both for their natural, as well as cultural, beauty. Over the course of his career, Jim has led major expeditions to Chile, Peru, Africa, Bhutan, China, India, Nepal, and Tibet. In 1989, he was the coleader of the initial ski expedition to the South Pole, the first overland crossing to the South Pole from the South American side. Because of his familiarity with the extreme landscape and hazards of the Antarctic, he was selected as one of the leaders for the first commercial crossing of South Georgia Island along the route taken by Ernest Shackleton on his epic *Endeavor* expedition. Jim has guided clients to Mt. Everest, Nupste, Lhotse, Mt. McKinley, Ama Dablam, Carstenz Pyramid, Elbrus, Aconcagua, and many more. His summit of Mt. Everest in 2000 with clients inspired him to become the first person to successfully guide all "Seven Summits," the highest point on each of the seven continents, in less than one year. Jim has been honored numerous times for his prowess and dedication: He received the National Park Service Search and Rescue Award in 2003; was named a member of the "Durable Dozen" in *Best Life* magazine (along with Ulysses S. Grant, Ernest Shackleton, and Chuck Yeager) for his Seven Summits guiding achievement; and recipient of the Explorer Club's prestigious Lowell Thomas Award in 2009. He is vice president of the American Mountain Guides Association and is an AMGA-certified alpine and rock guide.

If You Go

▶ **Getting There:** The eclectic tour of the Three Gorges of the Yangtze begins and ends in Shanghai, which is served from the U.S. by most international carriers.

▶ **Best Time to Visit:** Jim Williams would advise *now*, as there's no telling exactly how quickly the waters of the Yangtze will rise as a result of the dam.

▶ **Guides/Outfitters:** Exploradus Expeditions (307-733-8812; www.exploradus.com) can lead guests on a Three Gorges adventure on a customized basis.

DESTINATION

10

THE LOST CITY

RECOMMENDED BY **Nathaniel Waring**

For many, Colombia conjures up images of cocaine cartels and guerilla groups, sometimes working in tandem to create chaos. For Nathaniel Waring, Colombia means unblemished beaches along the southernmost shores of the Caribbean Sea and the amazing ruins found at *La Ciudad Perdida* . . . the Lost City. "The Lost City does not have as many buildings as Machu Picchu to the south in Peru," Nathaniel said. "But for me, it's equally as beautiful as the Incan settlement. The stonework is incredibly intricate, and the sight of perpetually snowcapped Pico Cristóbal Colón—Colombia's highest mountain at 18,701 feet—rising right above the steamy rainforest, is both transcendent and startling. The whole time you're there, your mouth is hanging open. Most important of all, there are very few people . . . very, very few, relative to the Inca Trail."

The Lost City—called "Teyuna" by the local people—was constructed by the Tayrona Indians sometime between the sixth and eleventh centuries (there is still debate on its inception, as archaeological research here has been less than exhaustive). In its heyday, Teyuna is believed to have served as a trading center, connecting the Incan empire in the Andes to the south with the Mayans to the north. At least several thousand Tayrona are believed to have lived here, forebears of the Kogi and Arsario Indians; some Kogi and Arsario still live near the ruins today. The city is carved into a mountainside at an elevation of approximately 3,500 feet; its plazas, terraces, and other structures were built from rocks hauled up from the Buritaca River, which has carved a large valley at the foot of the settlement. Much of the site has not been formally explored and remains shrouded in jungle overgrowth. "Lost," it should be mentioned, is something of a misnomer, as members of the Kogi, Arsario, and Arhuaco tribes have long known of the city's existence and tried to shield it from outsiders. It was "discovered" in 1975 by treasure seekers, who ransacked the site. Government presence at the Lost City in the form of a small military regiment has dissuaded other robbers.

Treks to the Lost City are generally done over six days, with three days heading in, a day to inspect the ruins, and two days to hike out. Treks generally stage near the coastal town of Santa Marta; all visiting groups must be accompanied by a Colombian guide. Though only fifteen miles each way and gaining less than 3,000 feet in elevation, the trek is fairly rigorous. "There's a good deal of up and down, and many stream crossings," Nathaniel recalled. "Thanks to the stream crossings and not infrequent rain, you're often wet. Plus, it's quite hot, and the mosquitoes and sand fleas can be very aggressive. But the jungle is beautiful—you're very aware of the remoteness of the place, where you can pick bananas from trees you pass. There are nice swimming holes in the Buritaca River at each of the overnight camps along the route, and strong Colombian coffee to get you started in the morning." Visitors will usually stop for a brief visit in a Kogi or Arsario village that's near the trail for a glimpse of these people's simple hunter-gatherer lives. (Some villagers act as porters, carrying food and other supplies into the camps for trekkers.) There's also another optional, unadvertised tour: Coca processors will approach visitors and offer to show you a primitive lab where cocaine paste is produced. (There is certainly an element of risk in a trek to the Lost City. Both Marxist guerillas and rightwing paramilitary groups have used the coca-rich region for narcotics processing, and in 2003, a group of tourists at the Lost City was kidnapped, though they were later safely released. Increased military presence in Sierra Nevada de Santa Marta National Park has undoubtedly made the region safer for visitors, but one should travel here with some discretion.)

Your travails in the jungle are well rewarded once you reach the base of the Lost City, though your work is not quite done. "You come out of the jungle to a vast series of steps, leading up from the river—1,200 in all," Nathaniel described. "Some are six feet wide, all are almost perfectly even. When you get to the top of the steps, there is a series of foundations—terracing for growing crops—that go up the side of the mountain for another three quarters of a mile. You're surrounded by stone constructions, and rising on three sides are incredibly steep and lushly forested hillsides, with waterfalls bursting out in all directions. There's a guide stationed at the Lost City—along with the soldiers who protect it from the looters, all young and, in my experience, quite friendly (though heavily armed)—and he will provide some history of the site. You can also explore on

11

DESTINATION

your own. The site is quite expansive; as you walk around, you realize that parts of the settlement have not yet been extracted from the jungle. The last time I was there, my group was the only tourist group present."

Visitors to the Lost City spend two nights in a modest camp, allowing a full day for exploration. Then you hike the same trail out . . . or, for a slightly different experience, you can helicopter out. "It's a small helicopter that's available for special charter," Nathaniel continued. "It has to be light enough to land on one of the foundations at the site, as the hillside is otherwise too steep for landing. As you take off, you're aware of how remote the city is; there's no construction for many miles, only jungle. You can't help but wonder why the Tayrona picked this remote site."

Those trekking to the Lost City may wish to leave a day or two to explore the beaches of nearby Tayrona National Park. This preserve encompasses fifty-eight square miles, stretching from Sierra Nevada de Santa Marta National Park through equatorial rain forest to a swath of marine habitat along the Caribbean. Tayrona is considered one of the Americas' most biologically diverse coastal zones and is home to jaguars, ocelots, red howler and lemurine owl monkeys, and some 300 recorded bird species, including guans and paujils; Andean condor and blue-billed curassows have also been spotted here. Idyllic palm-fringed beaches dot coves that are connected by trails slicing through the jungle. "The coastline is jagged, as if shaped by fjords," Nathaniel added. "It's reminiscent of Maine or Norway, though with tropical vegetation and warm translucent water instead of dense pine forests and freezing seas."

NATHANIEL WARING opened the first U.S.A. office of Cox and Kings in 1989, and served as the company's president. Since that time he has flown, kayaked, swum, hiked, biked, and surfed across much of Asia, India, Africa, and Latin America. Nathaniel has led exploratory trips to Ethiopia's Omo Valley, along the Rift Valley Lakes, and into the jungle and islands of Burma. He is listed by *Travel + Leisure* and *National Geographic Traveler* magazines as an expert on Africa and Peru. Waring sits on the advisory board of the Oberoi Group of Hotels. A competitive masters swimmer, he enjoys swimming around small islands such as North Island in the Seychelles, Reethi Rah in the Maldives, and, closer to home, Key West, Florida. Nathaniel recently retired from Cox and Kings, and is devoting more time to surfing, free diving, and the study of marine biology.

If You Go

▶ **Getting There:** Lost City treks generally stage in Santa Marta, which has air service from Bogotá on Avianca (866-998-3357; www.avianca.com).

▶ **Best Time to Visit:** Treks can be led to the Lost City year-round, though July and August tend to be a bit cooler and drier; spring and fall have the most precipitation.

▶ **Accommodations:** Lodging options in Santa Marta, the main staging area for Lost City treks are listed on www.santamartainfo.com.

▶ **Guides/Outfitters:** Currently, there are several guide services allowed to bring hikers to the Lost City, including Turcol Travel Agency (+57 5 4 21 22 56; www.buritaca2000 .com) and Sierra Tours (+57 5 4 21 94 01; www.sierratours-trekking.com). Nathaniel Waring (nathaniel86@mac.com) can arrange a hiking/helicopter excursion.

MAROON BELLS–SNOWMASS

NATIONAL WILDERNESS

RECOMMENDED BY **Margie Cohen**

The next time you visit your doctor's office, have a gander at the calendar of naturescapes hanging in the waiting room or above the examination table. You may come across a stunning shot of twin snow-flecked mountain peaks perfectly reflected in a calm lake. This would likely be the Maroon Bells, widely regarded as Colorado's most photographed scenic overlook.

Maroon Bells–Snowmass National Wilderness was the very first hiking venue that Margie Cohen visited, and after twenty-five years of hiking and trekking the world, it remains a favorite transformative place of hers. "I did not camp or hike as a kid," Margie recalled. "When I was a teenager, my aunt and uncle, who were ardent skiers, bought a second home in Aspen, Colorado. On my first summer visit, my cousin asked me to join him for a hike. I thought it would be a few miles, but what he had in mind was a backpacking trip. My aunt and uncle dropped us off at the Snowmass Creek trailhead, and off we went. I had no idea what I was in for. I had borrowed equipment, completely mis-fitted for my small size as well as ill-fitting hiking boots and poor rain gear. The first day, we hiked in to Snowmass Lake. Crossing a boggy area atop a beaver dam, I got totally soaked and was miserable. My cousin cooked mac and cheese for dinner—a food I detest but ate gratefully that evening. By the second day, as we climbed Buckskin Pass and proceeded down to Maroon Lake, I had a bandaged knee. Yet, despite my discomfort, that trip stuck with me. Something about being in that environment was spiritually transforming. I've visited the Maroon Bells every year thereafter, and it has impacted the direction of my life. A master's degree in business and a ten-year corporate career morphed into starting and owning an outdoor-outfitting business and then working for an environmental and recreation non-profit organization."

OPPOSITE: Maroon Bells (made up of Maroon Peak and North Maroon Peak) is one of America's most photographed mountains.

The Maroon Bells–Snowmass National Wilderness comprises more than 183,000 acres in the Gunnison and White River National Forests, just to the south and west of the alpine-skiing communities of Aspen and Snowmass. The park's namesake mountain (and the focal point of the aforementioned calendars) takes its name from the bell shape of its two peaks, Maroon Peak (14,156 feet) and North Maroon Peak (14,014 feet), and their distinctive red color, which results from the weathering of iron-bearing hematite present in the rock. Four other "fourteeners"—Castle Peak, Capitol Peak, Snowmass Mountain, and Pyramid Peak—rise within the boundaries of the wilderness area, part of the Elk Mountain range. "One of the qualities that make Maroon Bells a unique spot is that it's one of the few places that's accessible by car where you can have a high-alpine experience," Margie continued. "There's never full snow melt. In fact, Maroon Bells can get snow in August." That road access, which can bring tour buses from the Prada store in downtown Aspen to the banks of Maroon Lake in twenty minutes, can make for a shared alpine experience . . . at least for the first mile or so on the trail. "There's a modest day hike from Maroon Lake up to Crater Lake, four miles round-trip," Margie added. "On a recent visit, this stretch had a line of people, single file—there was no way to pass anyone. I wouldn't be surprised if the trail sees well over 500 people a day in the summer. But when you take the turnoff from this trail to reach Buckskin Pass, the crowds melt away."

There are one hundred miles of trails cut across the Maroon Bells, with many segments eclipsing 10,000 feet for miles at a time. An excellent two-day hike is Snowmass Creek, which showcases some of the region's most stunning Rocky Mountain panoramas. "On the second day, you leave Snowmass Lake and climb to Buckskin Pass, at close to 12,500 feet," Margie said. "At the top of the pass, you have 360-degree views—upward to several peaks (including Pyramid Peak, Snowmass Mountain, and Capitol Peak) as well as downward to Snowmass Lake." For a longer hike, one of Margie's favorites is Four Pass Loop, a twenty-four-mile walk that crosses Buckskin Pass, Trail Rider Pass, Frigid Air Pass and West Maroon Pass. "The window to do this hike is finite, as the high passes aren't clear of snow until around July and begin to close up in early September," Margie added. "The wildflowers in the meadows behind the Bells are jaw-droppingly beautiful. There's Indian paintbrush in every color—white, yellow, red, hot pink, purple, orange. The paintbrush is interspersed with purple and white columbine, Colorado's state flower, as well as daisies and sunflowers. All this unfolds before you from above tree line. It's an amazing viewscape—all you can see for ten miles are wildflowers, with snow-capped rocky spires in the background and the occasional glacier lake or tarn."

Another very popular hike is the Conundrum Creek Trail, which leads to wonderful backcountry hot springs. "It's eight miles in, and you go from 9,000 feet to 11,200 feet—fairly easy, at least by Colorado Rocky Mountain standards," according to Margie. "The hot springs are above tree line, and when a thunderstorm comes in, you don't want to leave yourself exposed, let alone be sitting in a pool of water.

"The last time I was there, there were a dozen people who had hiked in. As can happen, a severe thunderstorm came through, and one couple stayed in the water. With the frequency of the lightning, I thought there could be a direct strike. I spoke to the couple later that evening, and one of them said, "Oh! We didn't even know it stormed."

MARGIE COHEN is director of marketing and development for the American Hiking Society, where she supports the organization's corporate sponsors, donors, and foundations. Margie earned her BA from Tufts University and an MBA from the Kellogg School of Management at Northwestern University. She has more than twenty years of business experience, including ten years as a management consultant; she also started and operated an outdoor-outfitting business because of her commitment to "human-powered" outdoor recreation and desire to help connect people with nature. Margie has hiked throughout North America, South America, Europe, Australia (including New Zealand), and Asia (including Vietnam and Cambodia).

If You Go

▶ **Getting There:** Maroon Bells is near Aspen, Colorado, roughly a four-hour drive from Denver. Aspen receives direct flights from Frontier Airlines (800-432-1359; www.frontier airlines.com) and United (800-864-8331; www.united.com).

▶ **Best Time to Visit:** The window for hiking the high passes is from early July through late August.

▶ **Accommodations:** You'll find a list of campgrounds at the U.S. Forest Service Web site (www.fs.fed.us/r2/whiteriver). The Aspen Chamber of Commerce (800-670-0792; www .aspenchamber.org) can help with more opulent lodgings.

DESTINATION 12

VANOISE NATIONAL PARK

RECOMMENDED BY **Phyllis Grove**

"I wanted to do a four- or five-day hike on my own in the Alps," Phyllis Grove began. "In my research, I came across a description of the Tour des Glaciers in Vanoise National Park, in France. I had never done a hut tour in Europe, and this itinerary nicely matched my criteria. I started my adventure in the town of Pralognan-la-Vanoise, just outside the park, and it turned out that the gentleman who ran the *chambre d'hôte* where I stayed was an avid hiker. He introduced me to a number of excellent day hikes. It always impresses me how quickly you can get into stunning scenery from the towns that dot this region of the Alps. From Pralognan-la-Vanoise, you can come upon glaciers just two hours from town."

Vanoise National Park rests just south of its more well-known neighbor, Mont Blanc, in the Savoie region of France. The park was established in 1963 (making it France's first national park) to provide a sanctuary for the ibex, a mountain goat easily distinguished by its large, elaborately curved horns. Ibex were once common in the mountains of France and central Europe; it was ibex that were depicted in the famed cave paintings at Lascaux. The introduction of hunting by firearms in the 1700s nearly brought the animal to extinction, but in 1922, the Italian government provided a safe haven for the ibex by creating Gran Paradiso National Park, in the region of the Graian Alps, just east of what would become Vanoise. Together, Vanoise and Gran Paradiso comprise nearly 500 square miles of protected land, making it the largest such preserve in western Europe.

Vanoise is crisscrossed by almost 300 miles of trails, and includes more than 100 peaks that rise more than 10,000 feet—including Grande Casse, which reaches 12,647 feet. Two of the Alps' great long-distance trails—Grande Randonnées (GR) 5 and 55—weave through the park from north to south, en route to the Mediterranean Sea.

OPPOSITE:
In Vanoise,
hikers move
from barren tree-
strewn slopes to
verdant meadows
over the course
of a day's hike.

13

DESTINATION

Vanoise compresses many of the Alps' great attractions into a compact area. "Unlike Chamonix, Vanoise boasts multiple peaks, glaciers, and valleys," Phyllis continued. "There are interesting limestone rock formations—not like in Sedona, but still quite beautiful—and the contrast between barren, scree-strewn slopes on one hillside and verdant alpine meadows dotted with wildflowers on the other is very pleasing. You also have the flexibility to do shorter hut-to-hut hikes or a ten-to-twelve-day tour." Hikers in Vanoise are almost certain to encounter an ibex, as the park is now home to approximately 2,000 of the animals. (The ibex also graces the park's insignia.) Both males and females sport horns, though the appendages of male ibexes are much larger, sometimes reaching to more than a yard in length. Vanoise is also home to more than 5,000 chamois, a goatlike ungulate roughly half the size of the ibex, with distinctive black-and-white face markings.

Overnight tours for those visiting the Vanoise are on routes designed to bring sojourners from one of the seventeen huts operated by the park to another. (There are thirty-three other huts in the park operated by private entities or French hiking clubs.) Phyllis opted for the Tour des Glaciers, a roughly forty-five-mile one-way circuit that can be completed over four or five nights. As its name implies, this tour navigates around the park's signature glaciers, which are part of the largest remaining ice cap in Western Europe. The glaciers are in view throughout the hike. "None of the days were particularly grueling," Phyllis recalled. "It was nine or ten miles, with only a few big uphills each day. Though I was on my own, I felt very safe for most of the trip. The only time I was unnerved came at a point when I had to hike through a flock of sheep that were being guarded by Pyrenean mountain dogs. They're large animals, and though I didn't think they'd bite me, it was still unsettling to encounter them by myself."

The experience of hut (or refuge) hiking may be unfamiliar to some Americans, though it's quite the norm in the Alps. Instead of carrying your home on your back and making camp more or less where you please, you move on a regulated circuit from hut to hut, sacrificing a level of freedom and solitude, but likewise losing the weight of a tent and other backpacking accoutrements and gaining amenities such as bathrooms, mattresses, and, in some cases, hot tubs and saunas. If you're hut-hiking in Vanoise National Park, you can leave your freeze-dried food and camp stove behind. "Breakfast and dinner were served in each of the huts I stayed in," Phyllis continued, "and this being France, the food was fantastic. Each night there was a three-course dinner. Generally one menu is prepared. As I'm a vegetarian, my hosts were happy to make special meals for me."

"From an accommodations standpoint, there was a lot of variance from one hut to the next—and, for that matter, from the huts in one country to the next in the Alps. In one hut, each sleeping room had a piece of plywood with six mattresses laid out—the mattresses were more like chair pads. One of my plywood-mates snored—in fact, by the end of the night, all of my fellow hikers were snoring. Another night, I was woken up by the carryings-on of an amorous couple. [This is France!] On a later trip in the Dolomites, I learned that it was possible to have your own room."

While privacy may not be a big part of the Vanoise hut-hiking experience, splendid views are. "When I reached the last hut on my hike—Refuge du Col de la Vanoise—there was an incredible view of a mountain. I could've easily hiked out to Pralognan-la-Vanoise, but the perspective of the mountain was riveting. I watched it with a few of my fellow hikers as the sun was setting, with shadows settling over the massif. I continued watching as a full moon rose, eventually hanging above the peak."

PHYLLIS GROVE is marketing director for Mountain Hardwear, which designs, sources, and markets high-end mountaineering and outdoor equipment, apparel, and accessories. Before joining Mountain Hardwear, she held marketing positions with Procter and Gamble and Dreyer's Grand Ice Cream. An avid hiker, Phyllis has walked trails in the U.S., Scotland, France, Italy, Peru, Chile, Argentina, and Nepal.

If You Go

▶ **Getting There:** Visitors will generally fly into Geneva or Lyon, France, which are served by most major international carriers.

▶ **Best Time to Visit:** Trails are generally accessible from mid-June through mid-September.

▶ **Accommodations:** Reservations for the huts in Vanoise National Park can be made from May 15 on through Centrale de Reservation du Massif de la Vanoise (+33 5 49 08 71 49). Lodging options in Pralognan-la-Vanoise are highlighted at www.pralognan.com.

▶ **Guides/Outfitters:** The Companie des guides de la Vanoise website (www.cieguide vanoise.com) lists local guides. Many American adventure-travel companies lead trips to Vanoise National Park, sometimes as part of the Grande Traversée des Alpes.

PAYS BASQUE/PAÍS VASCO

RECOMMENDED BY **Tanya Nygaard**

Say "mountains of France," and most think immediately of the Alps. Say "people of France," and you'll likely picture . . . well, the French.

A visit to the Pays Basque region of southwesternmost France calls both preconceptions into question. "The Pays Basque region is in the foothills of the Pyrenees, and extends south of the border into Spain," Tanya Nygaard explained. "It's gorgeous country, quite varied—and largely undiscovered. On walks here, we move from the coast to the hillsides and back to the coast, with lots of charming hamlets along the way. In Pays Basque, you're hiking through steep valleys and rolling, verdant countryside. It's very different than the Alps, where so many of the trails are above tree line. A highlight of a walking trip here is the chance to get to know a bit about Basque culture. The Basque are very proud of their heritage, and they know that people from outside of their part of the world know little about them. It's believed that the Basque people—*Euskaldunak* in the Basque language—have inhabited the region along the western edge of the Pyrenees for thousands of years, perhaps as long as 35,000 years. They have a distinctive language, cuisine, and music, and are very excited to share Basque ways of life with visitors. The French have the phrase *joie de vivre*, but the Basque people seem to capture this spirit a bit more. They love to laugh and have fun."

A walk of the Pays Basque region might begin in the bustling market town of St-Jean-Pied-de-Port. Once a stopping point for Catholic pilgrims en route to Santiago de Compostela in Galicia, St-Jean-Pied-de-Port, with its pink sandstone houses and winding cobblestone lanes, is one of the Basque country's most picturesque towns. The central elements of any Basque village—the church, the *hôtel de ville* (town hall) and the *fronton* (pelota court) are all on display. Here you can enjoy your first Basque meal, from Michelin-

68

starred chef Firmin Arrambide. "Basque cuisine is spicier than most food in Europe," Tanya continued. "There's lots of lamb and lots of seafood, and many main courses are seasoned with peppers. You're also sure to come upon cherries and a fabulous cherry cake, *gâteau basque*, and sheep's-milk cheese, *petit basque*."

From St-Jean-Pied-de-Port, you can walk to Mount Arradoy. Passing through rolling farmland dotted with sheep, you'll come to the Irouléguy Vineyard on Arradoy's southern slope. Vines have been grown here since the twelfth century, and today the vineyard grows the grapes that typify the region—Courbus and Manseng for white wines, Cabernet and Tannat for reds. "The reds of Pays Basque are very hearty," Tanya added, "and pair wonderfully with lamb dishes." From Mount Arradoy, there are splendid views of northern Spain and the Pyrenees. Before leaving St-Jean-Pied-de-Port, you'll want to partake of a seminal Basque event—a pelota match. There are several variations of pelota, some that involve use of a racquet, some a basket, and some bare hands. Players on one team serve a hard rubber ball against a wall, while the opposing team attempts to return the serve as the ball bounces back; imagine a higher-speed, more exacting form of racquetball. (A version of pelota is played in some parts of the U.S. as jai alai.) "In the match we see, players use their hands," Tanya said. "The fans are as interesting as the match, as they're very spirited. The matches bring the villages together."

Tanya's path through the Pays Basque next crosses into Spain, via the Col de Roncevaux—or *Roncesvalles*, in Spanish. Roncesvalles has a rich history: It was here that King Charlemagne's army was defeated in 778 AD by Basque tribes; his nephew, Roland, was killed in the battle, which was memorialized in the epic poem "The Song of Roland" (though the poem makes Charlemagne's enemies at Roncesvalles Muslims). "Some of the local people say that on stormy nights, you can hear the call of Roland's horn echoing through the hills," Tanya said. Roncesvalles is also on El Camino de Santiago, the pilgrimage to Santiago de Compostela, where tradition has it that the bones of St. James are buried. El Camino de Santiago was one of the most important pilgrimages in medieval times, and was walked by millions of the faithful. "You can still meet pilgrims on the trail today," Tanya continued. "They have a scallop shell on the back of their backpack; common to the shores of Galicia, the scallop shell is a longstanding symbol of El Camino de Santiago. Though I'm not on a religious quest, I still find walking the trail spiritual. I feel a kinship with the pilgrims, the common bond of hikers." Before returning to France and making your way to the Bay of Biscay, you'll hike to the village of Zugarramurdi, whose

citizens were terrorized by the forces of the Inquisition in the early 1600s, accused of witchcraft. You can visit Las Cuevas de las Brujas (Caves of the Witches), the gathering spot of these reputed practitioners of black magic.

For much of the walk, one mountain—La Rhune—has been in view. Mount La Rhune has a rich place in Basque folklore; the presence of stone circles and dolmens suggests that the mountain was held sacred by Neolithic residents. According to one Basque legend, La Rhune was once blanketed with gold, but when thieves attempted to remove it by burning down all of the trees, the gold melted away. The summit was rumored to be another gathering place for witches, and local villages retained monks to live on the mountain to discourage black magic. Before leaving the Pays Basque, you'll have the opportunity to trek to the summit, at 2,970 feet. "From the top of La Rhune, you can look west out over the Atlantic Ocean," Tanya said, "and look east to survey every place that you've been during the week."

TANYA NYGAARD is the France regional manager for Backroads, an active-travel company. Tanya spent a good part of her formative years in Tunisia, Egypt, and Syria, before heading north to France and Belgium. Her parents may have dragged her off to Arkansas for a few years, however, Tanya never lost her love of France and all things European. "What I like best about active travel is the opportunity to enjoy new places at a slow pace, to soak in the sights, sounds, and smells that are unique to the area," Tanya said, "and the chance to delve into the culture at hand, whether it's chatting with a farmer working in the vineyards or making friends with the local *boulanger*, baking croissants."

If You Go

► **Getting There:** The Pays Basque can be reached from Paris by high-speed train to Biarritz, France, where many walks stage. Biarritz is served by several airlines, including RyanAir (www.ryanair.com).

► **Best Time to Visit:** The Pays Basque enjoys a mild climate year-round. Precipitation is highest in the winter months.

► **Guides/Outfitters:** Backroads (800-462-2848; www.backroads.com) offers walking tours of the Pays Basque, billeting guests in comfortable country inns along the way.

OPPOSITE: One of the delights of a walk through Pays Basque is the chance to visit the small villages that dot the hillsides and valleys.

DESTINATION 14

YR WYDDFA, SCAFELL, AND BEN NEVIS

RECOMMENDED BY **Pete Royall**

Great Britain may not have the world's tallest mountains nor its most exotic vistas, but its peaks have inspired more than a few lines of verse and have helped catapult some of its citizens to great climbing achievements further afield. Each of the tallest peaks in Wales, England, and Scotland—Yr Wyddfa (better known to non-Welsh speakers as Snowdonia), Scafell Pike, and Ben Nevis, respectively—has its own charms and challenges. British climber Pete Royall believes that the hikers and Anglophiles will be best served by ascending all three mountains, back to back. "Despite being relatively low in altitude when compared with the world's highest peaks, these are nonetheless real mountains, as many people have discovered, to their joy—and a few to their cost. For me, the experience of climbing all three is so much more than the sum of each individual climb. I've come to call it the Three Peaks Challenge."

Thanks to their relative proximity (Pete has clocked the distance among the peaks as 460 miles by road and 280 miles as the crow flies), some intrepid hikers will attempt to climb all three in one twenty-four-hour period—a feat that poses both physical and logistical challenges. "There's a minimum of 10,000 feet of ascent and descent and twenty miles of walking, not to mention all of that driving," Pete continued. "While it can be done, most visitors appreciate a more leisurely pace that allows them to get a taste of the local countryside. A week is about right, as it gives you a day for each hike, plus a chance to do a bit of sightseeing as you move from Wales to England and then north to Scotland."

Traveling from the south to the north, Three Peaks challengers will first visit Yr Wyddfa, in Snowdonia National Park. Located in northwest Wales, Snowdonia comprises more than 800 square miles of land that's held in mixed public and private own-

15

DESTINATION

ership; unlike a typical national park in the United States, Snowdonia includes a number of small towns, and is home to some 25,000 residents. Pete likes to base his Yr Wyddfa ascent in the hamlet of Beddgelert. "Welsh is the first language here, and the town takes its name from the faithful hound of Prince Llewellyn," Pete explained. "The legend goes that Llewellyn left his hound Gelert to guard his baby son as he went to hunt a wolf. When he returned, Gelert's mouth was covered in blood, and his son's diaper was nearby. Llewellyn stabbed Gelert in a rage, only to find his son safe and the carcass of a wolf moments later. I like to take guests to visit the site of Gelert's grave the day before our hike.

"Yr Wyddfa boasts stunning, rugged scenery. There are a number of routes to the top, and all the hiking is above tree line. My favorite is the Snowdonia Horseshoe, which traverses the ridges that enclose the high mountain lakes of Lynn Glas and Llyn Llydaw. This trail climbs the red rock pyramid of Crib Goch and runs along several knife-edge ridges. Near the top, the trail joins the tourist route—which includes a steam-powered railway, which has been bringing the less energetic to the summit since 1896. I like to take the Miners' Track down. This trail was built in the early 1800s for miners who extracted copper and slate from the region; the old workings of the mines can be seen from many trails. On the way back to town, I love to take visitors to the Pen-y-Gwryd hotel for a bit of refreshment. The Pen-y-Gwryd was home to the 1953 Everest team (that included Sir Edmund Hillary) as they prepared for their expedition on Yr Wyddfa."

From Snowdonia National Park, you'll head northeast into England, along the coast, past Liverpool, and on up to Lake District National Park, in the county of Cumbria. "If time permits, I suggest that visitors take a cruise from the southern end of Lake Windermere (the longest of the park's lakes) to the north and then drive across a high pass into the town of Keswick, which some might call the Aspen of England," Pete continued. "The Lake District can be described as a wheel, with Scafell Pike at the hub, and lakes radiating out; William Wordsworth first coined this description. For me, one of the region's great appeals is its scale. It's almost like a garden wilderness. In the valleys, you have charming towns maintained as they were 100 or 200 years ago, yet the high tops are still quite wild.

"You can climb Scafell from four different valleys, each with its own unique character and scenery. I like to approach from the north, via the burg of Seathwaite. You first ascend Glaramara (2,560 feet); if the weather is clear, you'll have a 360-degree panorama of the other peaks of the Lake District. Next, you'll cross a grassy ridge that connects to Allen Crags, then to Esk Hause. The *hause* (a Cumbrian word for "pass") brings you to the flanks of Ill Crag and boulder-strewn Broad Crag. After a bit of scrambling, you'll walk the last 300 feet to Scafell Pike (3,210 feet) itself, where you can look south to Wales and west to the sea and Ireland. I like to take the Corridor route down."

Leaving the Lake District, you'll follow the coast into Scotland, past Glasgow, along the shores of Loch Lomond and into the Highlands, where Ben Nevis—the tallest mountain in Great Britain (at 4,409 feet) awaits. "There's quite a contrast between the Lake District and the Highlands," Pete observed. "Where the Lake District is rather tame, Scotland is considerably wilder. There's much less of a sense of man having gotten control over the land. Ben Nevis has an interesting configuration. On the north side, there are tremendous cliffs that attract rock climbers from around the world, especially in the winter. The route that most people take is a series of zigzags on the south side. This trail was built over 200 years ago so pack animals could get supplies to the weather observatory near the summit, and became popular in the Victorian era when city dwellers were inspired to recreate in nature . . . and the railway came into existence to deliver them from London or Glasgow to Ben Nevis. I much prefer reaching the top by the Carn Mor Dearg arête, a spectacular ridge walk. As you're walking up the horseshoe-shape ridge, there are stunning views of the north face of the Ben and great vistas of the Cairngorms to the east. We take the normal route down."

Once you've descended Ben Nevis to complete the Three Peaks Challenge, the Nevis Inn awaits at trail's end, the perfect venue to enjoy a celebratory toast . . . perhaps a dram of one of Scotland's fine single-malt whiskeys.

PETE ROYALL was born and raised on Walney Island in Cumbria's South Lakeland. By the age of fourteen, he was spending most of his weekends exploring the mountains and valleys of Lake District National Park. By the age of sixteen, he had discovered the joys of granite, and his exploration grew to encompass climbing the crags and cliffs of mountain faces. Several seasons of climbing in the highlands of Scotland and the European Alps led to exploration in the Himalaya and, eventually, to most of the world's greater ranges. Since 1992, Pete has led treks and expeditions to the Nepal and Indian Himalaya, the Karakoram and Hindu Kush ranges of Pakistan and Afghanistan, and to the Andes. During this time, he has taken close to a hundred groups into the world's greater ranges for Britain's premier adventure-travel company, KE Adventure Travel, and has pioneered new routes in the Himalaya and the Karakoram mountains, including first-pass crossings and first ascents of unclimbed peaks. Pete also leads trips around Great Britain, including the Three Peaks Challenge.

If You Go

▶ **Getting There:** Following the itinerary set out above, you'll fly into Manchester, England, and drive west to Beddgelert, Wales. The trip concludes near Glasgow, Scotland. Both are served by most major international carriers.

▶ **Best Time to Visit:** June through September will find the weather most reliable.

▶ **Accommodations:** If you go it on your own, you may wish to stay in Beddgelert (www.beddgelerttourism.com); Keswick (www.keswick.org), and Glencoe (www.glencoescotland.com).

▶ **Guides/Outfitters:** Wandering Aengus Treks (888-811-4256; www.wanderingaengustreks.com) leads guests on the Three Peaks Challenge and handles all logistical details (transportation, lodgings, etc.).

15

DESTINATION

THE KALALAU TRAIL

RECOMMENDED BY **Charlie Cobb-Adams**

Kauai, Hawaii, is known—at least in promotional literature—as "The Garden Isle." As it turns out, sometimes travel brochures do not distort the truth. The oldest of the eight islands that make up the Hawaiian archipelago, Kauai's defining physical characteristic is Wai'ale'ale, a volcanic peak that rises from the center of this mountainous island. While not Kauai's highest mountain, Wai'ale'ale is responsible for capturing the moisture that makes the central part of the island one of the wettest places on earth, recording an average annual rainfall of 476 inches. In addition to supplementing Kauai's rich flora, eons of rain have carved some incredibly dramatic canyon landscapes, including the fabulous fluted cliffsides of Na Pali Coast State Park. Among the rugged cliffs rests the idyllic Kalalau Beach, which can only be reached by kayak or via the Kalalau Trail.

The Kalalau Trail begins at the terminus of the Kuhio Highway, in Ha'ena State Park, and passes through five valleys in Na Pali Coast State Park before reaching Kalalau Beach. En route it skirts dizzying sea cliffs (*pali* in Hawaiian), rushing streams, transcendent waterfalls, and primordial tropical forests. It only reaches the beach twice, but the powerful waves and currents here discourage swimming, however tempting. Though just eleven miles each way, the Kalalau Trail is considered one of the most demanding and potentially dangerous trails in the world. The strenuous nature of the trail comes from the accumulated elevation gain—some 5,000 feet—in the course of the walk. "The trail ascends from sea level to 800 feet in quite a few places," Charlie Cobb-Adams began, "and most people don't realize how much you work your 'negative' muscles on the downhill components, especially when you're carrying a fifty- or sixty-pound pack." The gains and descents are accentuated by the strength of the midday sun. The danger comes from the narrowness of the trail in many places, and the precipitous drops that await a misstep. "After the first two miles, the trail will become, at some places, just six to twelve inches wide," Charlie said. "What makes it even worse, right next to the trail there can be a 200-foot drop to the ocean. If you're hiking during the winter months, the trail can become very slippery and the potential for falling is even higher. I've seen waves at heights of twenty to forty feet crashing into the cliffsides and spraying up almost onto the trail!

Wild boars approaching 300 pounds and the occasional *pakalolo* (marijuana) farmer defending his crop round out the hazards awaiting hikers along the Kalalau Trail. As Charlie recommended, it makes good sense to *stay on the trail*.

Given the potential for misfortune, why do many ardent hikers make the trip to the northwest end of Kauai? Quite simply, it's the awesome beauty of the place. "Sierra Club ranked Kalalau Beach and Valley a 'ten' for beauty," Charlie added, "and Hollywood has filmed quite a few movies here—a *King Kong* movie, *Man with the Golden Gun*, and, most recently, *The Perfect Getaway*. I think the Hollywood treatment definitely draws people here." Some come for indefinite (and illegal) stays: Stories abound of hippie types who have established hidden gardens in Kalalau Valley, subsisting on vegetables and fruit and evading rangers, unable to pull themselves away from this paradise.

Visitors to Kalalau Beach are closely regulated, and those lucky enough to get a permit to hike here are only allowed five days. For many who've done the hike, the appeals of Kalalau Beach and Valley are powerful enough to egg on weary legs to attempt to complete the walk in one day. However, this task will prove daunting for all but the most athletic sojourners. There are several camping spots along the route to break the hike into segments. The first comes just two miles in from the trailhead at Ke'e Lagoon, at Hanakapi'ai Beach. "The waterfall near Hanakapi'ai is one of the most beautiful along the trail," Charlie opined, "falling approximately 500 feet, with a big pool at the bottom. I don't swim there because of falling rocks, but I will swim in the smaller pools prior to the big one." The more frequented campsite for those breaking their hike into segments is at Hanakoa, a classic hanging valley; a brief but difficult walk from here takes you to spectacular Hanakoa Falls. At Kalalau, the primary camping areas adjoin shaded beaches.

Almost anyone who has hiked the Kalalau Trail will speak to a certain mysticism that seems to hang in the air here among these awesome cliffs and mist-shrouded mountains; local people refer to this as *mana*, or big medicine. "Hiking the trail, I have heard the sound of humpback whales slamming the water with their tails," Charlie recalled. "The sound travels into the valleys, echoing like ancient drums to help me keep pace on the

trail to reach Kalalau by nightfall!" Some Kalalau visitors attain a heightened sense of consciousness with a little "medicinal" assistance. "When I do search-and-recovery missions, I find a lot of Hindu and other spiritual texts hidden away," Charlie said. "Some of the people who hide out in the valley call it the Eye of the Universe—though what that means, I can't tell you. I've heard from a number of reliable sources that there's a place in the valley called Smoke Rock where the Eye of the Universe people go to smoke *pakalolo*. On one occasion as they were smoking and praying, they looked up into the night sky and saw an image of Jesus Christ as a bright light coming toward them from the heavens.

"I don't know whether this is true or not, but I do know there's some kind of spiritual force out there."

CHARLIE COBB-ADAMS's family heritage on Kauai and the Kalalau Valley goes back more than a thousand years. He has been hiking, hunting, and exploring throughout the islands since he was thirteen years old. Charlie has worked for the Department of Land and Natural Resources Forestry and Wildlife Division, as well as the Parks Division in Hawaii, building and maintaining trails and leading missing-person searches along the Na Pali coast. He and his wife, Tanya, established Native Hawaiian Conservation and Hiking Expeditions in 1999 to share the natural wonders of Kauai with visitors.

If You Go

▶ **Getting There:** Kauai's Lihue airport is served by many carriers, generally through connecting flights from Honolulu or Maui, Hawaii.

▶ **Best Time to Visit:** Spring and summer are generally drier, with more reliable conditions overall. Information on obtaining permits is available from the Hawaii Department of Land and Natural Resources (www.hawaii.gov/dlnr).

▶ **Accommodations:** The Kauai Visitors Association (800-262-1400; www.kauaidiscovery .com) provides a comprehensive listing of accommodations on the Garden Isle.

▶ **Guides/Outfitters:** Charlie Cobb-Adams's company, Native Hawaiian Conservation and Hiking Expeditions (808-652-0478; http://nativehawaiianecotours.com), leads customized hikes on the Kalalau Trail.

OPPOSITE:
The Kalalau Trail
hugs the western
coast of Kauai,
above the famed
Na Pali cliffs.

DESTINATION 16

PUU KUKUI WATERSHED PRESERVE

RECOMMENDED BY **Jeff Wallach**

"If you're the sort of person who'd like to attempt what may be the least-traveled day hike on the planet, don't worry about visiting Bhutan or Ulaanbataar," Jeff Wallach declared. "Just book a flight to the Hawaiian Island of Maui, and start saving your money. And cross your fingers that you'll be one of the dozen folks given the opportunity to partake of the once-a-year hike through the Puu Kukui Watershed Preserve."

The eight islands that make up the Hawaiian archipelago boast the world's largest proportion of known endemic plant and animal species. Puu Kukui is an oasis on an island that many mainlanders already consider to be a paradise, a 8,340-acre private enclave that preserves a portion of Maui's tropical rainforest in perpetuity. Puu Kukui (meaning "hill of enlightenment" in Hawaiian) was established in 1988, set aside from the holdings of Maui Land and Pineapple Company [ML&P]. The preserve contains the summit of Mauna Kahalawai (elevation 5,788), which is one of the wettest places on earth, sometimes receiving as much as 600 inches of rain a year. Puu Kukui's unique ecosystem supports life found nowhere else in the world.

Before he even set foot in the helicopter that would spirit him toward the summit, Jeff was made aware of just how fortunate he was to gain access to Puu Kukui. "The photographer who accompanied me on the hike, Ron Dahlquist, turned to me before we got on the helicopter," Jeff recalled. "He said, 'You're a lucky man. I've been trying to get up here for fifteen years. And I know the president of the Maui Land and Pineapple Company.' ML&P has kept the general public at arm's length for the preserve in part to honor the native Hawaiian land management practice of *ahupua'a*, in which the islands are divided into wedges—defined by perennial streams—that reach from mountain summits down to the reefs. This model calls for caring for each wedge in a sustained and holistic way."

OPPOSITE:
The lucky hiker
who lands a
chance to hike
in the Pu'u
Kukui Water-
shed Preserve
frequently treads
on boardwalks
constructed to
protect rare flora.

The adventure at Puu Kukui begins with the donning of yellow rubber rainsuits and tall rubber boots, an intimation of the weather to come. "Ten minutes later, the helicopter was ascending past fields of ripening pineapples into a fast-moving river of clouds rippling above a wild and foreboding alpine environment," Jeff continued. "Canyons and waterfalls flew past beneath us. In the distance, aureoles of light occasionally reminded me that somewhere nearby, perfectly normal folks were slathering on sunscreen and snorkeling in the blue sea. A ways up the mountain, the nose of the helicopter swung from side to side in strong gusts above a tiny platform that we seemed unlikely to hit— but after a few tense moments, we managed to land on it with a loud thump. Though the annual Puu Kukui hikers are usually flown to the summit to descend several miles through cloud forest to this platform at a spot called First Bog, 4,500 feet above sea level, weather didn't permit our group to fly any higher. We'd get to climb the last 1,500 feet of elevation and then come back to First Bog to meet the helicopter . . . or hike additional miles downhill to a spot where a truck could scoop us up. I was struck by the air, which was like another atmosphere altogether from the beach. It was like inhaling pure, chilled oxygen."

All hiking in Puu Kukui is done on a narrow boardwalk built to protect the soil from disturbance that might permit unwanted plant life to take root—and to keep hiking boots above the preserve's montane bogs. "It's a cross between hiking and tightrope walking," Jeff described. "Several times during my hike, strong gusts of wind blew me off the boardwalk into the bog. Some experts estimate that each foot of bog here represents about 10,000 years of vegetative growth!" Thanks to steady trade winds, much of the flora in the upper reaches of Puu Kukui has evolved to grow close to the ground, some in miniature form. "The ohia trees usually grow from forty to seventy feet in height," Jeff added. "In Puu Kukui it barely manages twelve inches. As we made our way toward the top of the trail, our guide, Hank Oppenheimer (one of the conservationists that oversees the preserve), pointed out a rare native daisy, an endangered plant called snakeroot, and explained the potential for some of the endemic plants here to form the basis of new pharmaceuticals."

After a lunch of smoked marlin and chocolate biscuits in a crude shelter at the top of the trail ("Hank called it the 'Puu Kukui Hilton,'" Jeff shared), the group began the hike down. Heavy weather closed in as they descended—a fairly common occurrence—and with any helicopter landings out of the question, the group was able to experience some of the preserve's lower reaches. "The boardwalk gave way to a swampy trail that often showed glimpses of steep drops into deep bowls of unbroken forest on each side," Jeff said. "Whereas the upper reaches of Puu Kukui were open and windblown, the lower 'forest' was tight, almost Hobbit-like. Trees were furred with vegetation. The route reminded me of a backcountry climbers' trail where the word 'trail' is almost meant sarcastically.

"Steering clear of the wire traps set to ensnare wild pigs, slogging through mud, down-climbing slippery rocks and limboing beneath overhanging limbs, I took in the sweet smell of the jungle. In this pristine, primitive jungle, I half expected to come upon a triceratops snacking on the dense foliage. Anything seemed possible."

JEFF WALLACH is an award-winning author of five books, including *Beyond the Fairway* and *What the River Says*. He is also the cofounder and editor of TheAPosition.com, a golf and travel lifestyle Web site. Jeff has published more than 600 articles, essays, and features in magazines such as *Sports Illustrated*, *Men's Health*, *Men's Journal*, *GOLF*, *Golf Digest*, *Travel & Leisure Golf*, *Continental Airlines*, and many others. Jeff believes he is the only writer to ever sell the same story to *Popular Science* and *Seventeen* magazines. He is also cofounder of The Critical Faculty, a golf and travel consulting firm, and has done branding and marketing for many clients in the golf and travel industries. Jeff lives with his wife in Portland, Oregon, where he golfs, bikes, hikes, plays squash and soccer, and takes a lot of ibuprofen. He claims to have a pretty good short game for a journalist.

If You Go

▶ **Getting There:** Maui is served by many leading U.S. airlines and international carriers, including Hawaiian Airlines (800-367-5320; www.hawaiianair.com).

▶ **Best Time to Visit:** The only time to visit Puu Kukui is the one day a year hiking spots are offered to roughly a dozen people as part of a fund-raiser for a local charity. For details, please email the preserve's manager, Randy Bartlett, at rbartlett@mlpmaui.com.

▶ **Accommodations:** Kapalua Resort (800-527-2582; www.kapalua.com) is fairly close to the preserve, and offers upscale accommodations. The Maui Visitors Bureau (www.visit maui.com) offers a comprehensive list of lodging options.

DESTINATION 17

TORFAJÖKULL

RECOMMENDED BY **Dick Phillips**

When Dick Phillips first began leading walking tours to the region of Torfajökull in southern Iceland in the early 1960s, there was no name for the area. "Torfajökull is actually the name of a small ice cap," Dick began. "I just started calling the larger region Torfajökull, as I realized that my guests would not know the difference, and some name would be better than none at all. In the early days, we'd go for two weeks in the summer without seeing anyone else. The only people who visited the area were the shepherds who brought their sheep to graze in the spring and retrieved them in the fall. It's not quite as isolated now, though it's still very remote country with a great variety of terrain."

Iceland is nothing if not dramatic—a land of fire and ice, of stark, treeless landscapes and a rich mythical folklore that's still quite alive among Icelanders. The fire comes from the island's pronounced geothermal activities, which provide a considerable amount of heat and hot water for Iceland's 300,000-plus residents, and from the island's more than two dozen active volcanoes. The ice comes from glaciers, which have carved many fjords along the 3,000-mile coastline and constitute 11 percent of the nation's landmass. Much of Iceland was formed (and is forming) from volcanic flows, which explains some of its rugged topography. The birch trees that once covered one third of the island were cut to make way for sheep grazing, and for the most part have not been replaced. (Icelanders have two sayings about trees. One goes, "There is a naked woman behind every tree in Iceland." The other is, "If you ever get lost in the Icelandic National Forest, all you have to do is stand up!") As for myths and sagas, it seems that every landmark has a supernatural as well as a natural explanation. Most of the population lives on or near the coastline, which is warmed by the North Atlantic Drift Current, making it far more habitable than Greenland, 180 miles to the west.

OPPOSITE:
The Ófærufoss waterfall is one of the strange wonders you'll encounter on a trek through Torfajökull.

The Torfajökull wilderness encapsulates many of Iceland's most unique features. There are mountains, fells, glaciers, wild rivers, and, of course, abundant geothermal activity in the shape of geysers and hot springs. "Torfajökull is the most powerful thermal region in the country, and still untapped," Dick explained. "Around the ice cap (which peaks at 3,280 feet) I've counted seventeen big steam vents all visible from one point. The noise the steam vents generate is impressive, and you find yourself walking through thick clouds of steam. When you're away from the steam vents, the views from the ice cap can span the whole of Iceland's south and central interior. On a clear day, you can take in nine separate ice caps."

The two-week trek around Torfajökull favored by Dick is strenuous by most standards. While the rigors of high altitude are not an impasse, there are a number of rivers to cross, an average of eleven or twelve miles of walking a day and no support vehicles. Your accommodations will be a series of huts, some built over the years by Dick and his associates. The huts will not be mistaken for the more opulent offerings available on some trails in the Alps—some are made, in part, of turf and have dirt floors. A trek through Torfajökull is a dance between landscapes of sublime austerity—monochromatic lava fields framed by distant glaciers—and phenomena that border on the fantastical. "We move from a desertlike environment that's covered in volcanic ash—tephra," Dick continued. "There's no vegetation at all. Soon the tephra gives way to thick moss, then the landscape returns to a stony desert, and eventually it begins greening up again. Toward the end of the trek, we're in rolling, grass-covered hills. Along the way, there are mountains and plateaus of brilliantly hued rhyolite. Sometimes the rock is yellowish, sometimes green, sometimes orange. When the sun shines on it, it's magnificent. People think that the color is an achievement of a chemist, not nature. There are also vast deposits of obsidian." Other wonders you'll come upon include the stupendous Markarfljót Gorge; Eldgja, the largest volcanic canyon in the world; and its magnificent double waterfall, Ófærufoss.

Despite Torfajökull's ever-present geothermal activity, it would be a misconception to think that you can hike from hot spring to hot spring, having a relaxing bath every few hours. Yet several opportunities are presented in the course of your adventure. The first is at Strutslaug, a hot-spring oasis set among grassy hillsides near the end of your trek. There are several layover days here, giving you the chance to mix day hikes with natural-spa treatments. En route to the airport and your departure from Iceland, you may wish to partake of the Blue Lagoon, a man-made pool of mineral water that exists courtesy of the

Svartsengi geothermal power plant. The water that fills the lagoon, pumped up from a mile below, is the off-flow from Svartsengi, and takes its otherworldly hue—somewhere between antifreeze and a slushie—from high levels of silica and sulfur. It's surrounded by lava fields, and looks completely at home amid Iceland's topography—it's hard to believe it's man-made!

DICK PHILLIPS's love affair with Iceland began with his first visit, a month-long cycling tour in 1955. After his ninth visit, he set up a travel business in 1960 dedicated to Iceland, and has been organizing and leading walkers, cyclists, mountaineers, and kindred travelers ever since. In his more than fifty years devoted to Icelandic adventure, Dick opened the Fljótsdalur Youth Hostel, has discovered new and unused routes through the mountains, and has built a sterling reputation as a reliable and straight-dealing authority on what he calls "a land of challenge."

If You Go

▶ **Getting There:** Iceland Air (800-223-5500; www.icelandair.us) offers service from several U.S. cities to Reykjavik. From here, it's eighty to one hundred miles by car to the beginning of your trek.

▶ **Best Time to Visit:** Despite its northern location, Iceland has a temperate climate and can be enjoyed year-round. Most hikes in the Torfajökull region are led from mid-May through August.

▶ **Accommodations:** Visitors will generally overnight in Reykjavik upon arrival and before departure. Lodging options are outlined at the Iceland Tourist Board Web site (www.icelandtouristboard.com).

▶ **Guides/Outfitters:** Dick Phillips (+44 1434 381 440; icelandick@nent.enta.net) organizes walking tours of the Torfajökull. Sherpa Expeditions (+44 20 8577 2717; www.sherpaexpeditions.com) also manages bookings.

DESTINATION 18

THE AMALFI COAST

RECOMMENDED BY **Roberto Strippoli**

The mountainous Amalfi Coast has drawn visitors for centuries to gape at its incomparable vistas of olive groves and azure seas, inhale the scent of ripe lemons, and celebrate the gastronomic delights of this most abundant paradise. Few tourists, however, are aware of the paths that course through these hillsides, paths once used by pilgrims and merchants. "Hiking is unusual for most Italian tourists," Robert Strippoli began. "They visit the Amalfi Coast, but don't necessarily hike, so the trails are not crowded. Walking around Amalfi, you always have incredible vistas—the Gulf of Salerno to the south and west, the mountains above you, and small, brightly colored villages scattered among the hills. When you enter the villages, you have the added bonus of spending time with the delightful people—warm, friendly, and funny. And, of course, there's the food."

The *Costiera Amalfitana* rests south of Naples, along the southern edge of the Sorrento Peninsula. When leading his walking tours of greater Amalfi, Roberto likes to begin near the city of Sorrento, at Sant'Agata, in the town of Massa Lubrense. "Sant'Agata is at the very top of an incline between Amalfi and the Sorrentine Peninsula," Roberto continued. "You have views of Amalfi to the south, the island of Capri to the west, and Mount Vesuvius to the north. Walking down the incline through the area of Colli delle Fontanelle and Torca, you're introduced to the flora of the Mediterranean Sea—and the wonderful smells of the plants." The next stop on your preamble to Amalfi is Capri, an island that's attracted the rich and famous for millennia. The Roman emperor Tiberius was an early enthusiast, building a number of villas on the island and eventually administrating his kingdom from its shores. (Pop royalty who currently own property on Capri includes Mariah Carey.)

While perhaps better known for its people-watching and shopping opportunities, there are several interesting walks on Capri. One short but challenging hike is the

OPPOSITE:
A walk along
the Amalfi Coast
highlights the
region's colorful
coastal villages,
including Ravello.

Phoenician steps. "The steps lead from the main port on Capri—Marina Grande—to the island's other town, Anacapri," Roberto continued. "There are somewhere between 840 and 970 steps carved into the rock—I've never been able to count accurately while I'm leading guests! As you're climbing, you look down on the town of Capri below to the right and up to the rock promontory of Punta del Capo, where Villa Jovis, one of Tiberius's grand structures, remains." If time permits, you may wish to visit the Grotta Azzura, a sea cave that may have served as Tiberius's private swimming pool (and is certainly one of Capri's main tourist attractions).

From Capri, it's a quick boat ride to the mainland and the towns of the *Costiera Amalfitana*—including Positano, Amalfi, and Ravello. From these picturesque villages carved into the hillsides above the crashing surf, Amalfi's best hikes unfold. The first is The Path of the Gods. "This is, without question, my favorite walk around Amalfi," Roberto enthused. "You feel like you're walking through the clouds, suspended between sky and sea." The trail traverses the limestone hills midway between the peaks of the Lattari Mountains—Mount Tre Calli, Mount Catiello, and Mount San Michele—and the Gulf of Salerno, running between the village of Nocelle in the west and Bomerano in the east. You'll wander past terraced gardens of lemons, nuts, and grapes, rock archways, and flora that includes wild arugula, entranced by the contrasting blues of sky and sea. Another noteworthy hike that takes you away from the coast, but deep into the history of Amalfi, is the *Valle dei Mulini*, or Valley of the Mills. "Amalfi was once known for its paper production (*Carta d'Amalfi*)," Roberto added, "and this trail takes walkers along Canneto Creek, where the paper mills were situated to take advantage of water power. The mills are not in very good condition now, though it's easy to imagine how they might have once worked." This hike is nicely shaded most of the way, and the sound of distant waves crashing is replaced with running river water. (Those curious about the ancient paper-making process can visit the Museo della Carta near the bottom of the valley.)

After conquering the Path of the Gods or the Valley of the Mills, you will have earned a modest reward. In this part of the world, rewards often come in the form of food— perhaps a bowl of homemade *scialatielli* pasta (a cross between spaghetti and linguini) with shellfish, octopus, or *pezzogna* (a variety of sea bream popular in the region), and freshly picked vegetables. Your culinary experience on the Amalfi Coast reaches a climax during your cooking class with Mamma Agata. "Mamma Agata is a traditional southern Italian *mamma*," Roberto explained. "Short, chubby, hot-tempered, though quick to have

DESTINATION 19

her anger appeased. She used to cook for a wealthy American lady who lived on the coast, and frequently prepared meals for the lady's Hollywood guests—Frank Sinatra and Elizabeth Taylor, among others. Her daughter, Chiara, came from a stay in Ireland and realized that she had a treasure in her house—her mom. Soon after, the cooking school was born. The first year, they had four clients. The next year, four hundred."

Mamma Agata conducts her cooking classes in Ravello. "She doesn't speak English at all, though she understands everything English guests say," Roberto continued. "She cooks using all local ingredients. She'll fry traditional vegetables for a first course, then a pasta dish, then perhaps fish or chicken, often with lemons, and some cakes at the end. Guests are welcome to participate in preparing the dishes, then everyone eats together on the terrace, which is surrounded by ceramics and lemon trees, with expansive views of the coast. You have to eat the whole meal, or Mama won't let you leave."

ROBERTO STRIPPOLI was born and raised in Puglia (the heel of the boot of Italy), and is a trip specialist for Backroads, focusing on Italy. An avid biker and hiker, Roberto is eager to promote tourism in his homeland. When he's not leading walking tours, he runs a sailboat rental company—Vento di Puglia—with his brother, Francesco.

If You Go

▶ **Getting There:** Visitors will generally fly into Naples, Italy which is served by many international carriers, including Alitalia (800-223-5730; www.alitalia.com).
▶ **Best Time to Visit:** The climate on the Amalfi Coast is amenable to year-round hiking, though late spring and early fall offer the both mild temperatures and clear skies.
▶ **Accommodations:** There are many lodging options in the towns here, including in Positano, Ravello, and Amalfi. You can explore possibilities at www.amalficoast.com.
▶ **Guides/Outfitters:** Many adventure-travel companies lead trips along the Amalfi Coast, including Backroads (800-462-2848; www.backroads.com).

19

DESTINATION

THE NAKASENDO TRAIL

RECOMMENDED BY **Matt Malcomson**

"Though I'm a native of England, I've been fascinated with Japan for a long time," began Matt Malcomson. "I'm fluent in Japanese, I lived in the country for ten years, and have traveled the nation extensively. One of the places I was very eager to explore when I first moved to Japan was the Nakasendo Trail, which I'd heard a great deal about. It's not a hiking trail per se, but a historic route linking Tokyo with Kyoto, weaving through the mountains of the interior. Many outsiders picture Japan as a heavily industrialized place, a land of sprawling cities, bullet trains, and high-rise buildings. In reality, Japan is 80 percent mountains, and here the influence of modernity is much less pronounced. Some of the Nakasendo has been consumed by the cities, but there are still sections that exist much as they did hundreds of years ago. These are the portions I like to walk."

The Nakasendo Trail was established in Japan's feudal period, and dates back to the eighth century. Known as the "path through the mountains," the Nakasendo is a 350-odd-mile "highway" that once delivered samurai, merchants, feudal lords, and other assorted travelers to Edo (Tokyo) and back. Sixty-nine post towns dot the trail, resting spots where sojourners could partake of a meal, a hot bath, and a night's rest. A handful of towns have been preserved (and, in some cases, restored) to their eighteenth- or nineteenth-century state, and three such towns are in the Kiso Valley, which unfolds along Japan's Kiso Mountains. "I like to focus on walks in this region, both for the character of the towns—among them, Magome, Tsumago, and Narai—and for the walk itself," Matt said. "There's some on-road walking, but also trails through the forest, dirt trails in the mountains, and old cobblestone paths in the villages. We pass through beautiful bamboo forests; walk in the shadow of 5,371-foot Mount Komagatake as you cross the Torii Pass; wander along rice paddies, cherry orchards, and modest fields planted with leeks and green tea; and pass tumbling waterfalls. The contrasts are very pleasing. And by moving at a slow pace, visitors get excellent insight into Japanese culture."

Matt's preferred path begins in the town of Niekawa, the first of eleven post towns in the Kiso Valley; from here, you'll walk to Narai, then on to Yabuhara, next to Tsumago. Walks will generally conclude in Magome, though the trail to Kyoto continues for 125 more miles. (To bypass more developed areas of the trail and make the most of the historical sections, most visitors will take trains at various points in their trip.) "Many Japanese will do the whole walk over the course of many years, a week at a time," Matt added. "The Nakasendo Trail, and particularly these villages, are of very great interest to Japanese tourists. In fact, they are often visited by tour buses, the way Americans might visit Gettysburg or Brits might visit Stratford-upon-Avon. I like to stay overnight in these places, as most of the domestic tourists don't arrive until nine A.M., and they go home at five P.M. In the early morning and evening, you have the places to yourself."

Your accommodations along the Nakasendo Trail help define the experience, transporting you to a simpler time of traveling samurai. Guests stay in *ryokans* (Japanese-style country inns) or *minshukus* (the equivalent of bed-and-breakfasts), generally run by a family. Sleeping quarters are spartan by most standards; at some *minshukus*, guests are taken aback to find their rooms completely empty! (Don't worry; futons, which are used in lieu of beds, are stored in the room's closet.) Meals, which are generally included in your room fee, are a highlight. "*Ryokans* and *minshukus* distinguish themselves by their meals—fabulous, multicourse affairs," Matt explained. "Japan has a strong sense of regional cuisine, and when domestic tourists visit the Kiso Valley, they're eager to sample local fare. This might mean *sansai*, or mountain vegetables—cooked fern for example, that's gathered in the morning and prepared that evening, and *iwana* (river fish). Dinners usually consist of individual courses that include pickles, a grilled fish, a grilled meat, tempura, raw fish, rice, and soup—all served in the ambience of a lovely old wooden home."

The post town of Tsumago may best capture the spirit of Japan's Edo period, which spanned from 1603 to 1868. The town has been painstakingly preserved—cars are banned from main streets and phone and power lines are concealed. "Tsumago is a living museum," Matt enthused. "Many people still live in *machiya*, traditional town houses. These dwellings have very narrow fronts on the street, but are very long. That's because in feudal times, homes were taxed on street frontage." Tsumago's *Honjin* (principal inn, reserved for government officials and wealthy travelers) and *Wakihonjin* (for less-well-heeled sojourners) have also been preserved. Looking out across the Kiso Valley from the former site of Tsumago Castle, it's not hard to imagine samurai or lords looking out upon the same vista two or three hundred years ago.

Hot baths are an essential component of Japanese life, and for Matt, one of the highlights of any visit. "Bathing is almost a religious experience in Japan," he continued. "Shintoism holds cleanliness very highly, and the ritual of bathing goes to the core of Japanese life. There are more than 3,000 named hot springs (*onsen*) in Japan thanks to all the volcanic activity, and though there are no hot springs in Narai, Tsumago, or Magome, there are still hot baths. At the *ryokan*s and *minshuku*s, the baths are segregated by sex. There's a tiled area where individuals can sit and rinse off in a shower, and then enter the bath for soaking. Baths—which are not terribly hot, at about 40 degrees Celsius (104 degrees Fahrenheit)—are almost always a postdinner affair."

MATT MALCOMSON is managing director of Oxalis Holidays, a travel company specializing in tours of Japan and Armenia. He first traveled to Japan at the age of eighteen, and has been exploring the archipelago ever since, living in Nara, Miyazaki, and Tokyo for ten years, working for an international magazine, leading outdoor trips, and travel writing. Matt became interested in Armenia in the 1990s while traveling in the region, and soon became involved in a sustainable-tourism project while studying the Armenian language. He leads trips in both Japan and Armenia.

If You Go

▶ **Getting There:** The itinerary described above begins in Tokyo and ends in Kyoto, which is best served by the Kansai International Airport in Osaka, Japan.

▶ **Best Time to Visit:** The Kiso Valley region can be visited year-round, though June through September can be uncomfortably wet, warm, and humid.

▶ **Accommodations:** If you go it alone, reservations for minshukus can be made by contacting the tourist offices in Magome (+81 264 59 2336) and Tsumago (+81 264 57 3123). Be advised that many *minshuku* owners do not speak English.

▶ **Guides/Outfitters:** A number of travel companies lead tours along the Nakasendo Trail, including Oxalis Adventures (+44 20 7099 6147; www.oxalis-adventures.com).

ACADIA NATIONAL PARK

RECOMMENDED BY **Sheridan Steele**

"There are two aspects of Acadia National Park that make it wonderfully appealing to hikers, and unique among other parks," longtime National Park Service executive Sheridan Steele began. "First, there's the tremendous variety of hiking opportunities available within the confines of a relatively small space. Acadia has 120 miles of trails, not including the carriage roads, and they take you along mountain summits, along lakes, above the rugged coastline—even across tidal flats. The diversity of vistas of this lovely stretch of coastal land is staggering. The second thing that's distinctive about Acadia is the rich history of the trail system. Many were built by groups of local citizens under the auspices of "village-improvement societies" years before Acadia received its National Park designation. The citizens' goal was to give visitors more opportunities to interact with the natural world. Many of the trails that were built would not be built today, as they'd never meet safety and environmental protection criteria. Where modern trails would switchback through steeper areas, these trails go straight up; you climb on iron rungs and walk around exposed cliffs, holding on to iron railings. You have wonderful vistas when you get to the top of these trails, but the experience of climbing itself is very rewarding."

Most of Acadia National Park's granite headlands, rocky beaches, and spruce-fir forests are contained on Mount Desert Island, approximately three quarters of the way up Maine's sprawling coastline, and about an hour's drive southeast from the city of Bangor. Acadia was the first national park established east of the Mississippi River, and its millions of annual visitors have the painters of the Hudson River School, at least in part, to thank. The painters Frederic Church and Thomas Cole (among others) captured the region's beauty for city dwellers in the south, helping to draw the then-developing leisure class up north

from Philadelphia, New York, and Boston. The affluent of the Gay Nineties (including the Rockefellers, Vanderbilts, and Carnegies) built grand estates on the island, decamping there for a portion of each summer. While the robber barons changed the social face of Mount Desert Island, they were instrumental in setting aside the land that would eventually become a national park in 1919. Fearing the onslaught the surrounding woodlands would face with the development of a mobile gasoline-powered sawmill, the summer citizenry was galvanized under the leadership of Charles Eliot and George B. Dorr, who spearheaded preservation efforts; Dorr and would become the park's first superintendent. (John D. Rockefeller contributed another signature facet of the park: its forty-five miles of broken-stone carriage roads, so popular with equestrians and bicyclists.)

Many visitors to Acadia will take in Cadillac Mountain (named for an early French settler, not the automobile), one of the first points in the United States to be touched by the sun's rays each morning, or Somes Sound, a fjordlike bay cut into the granite on Mount Desert's south-central coast. Hikers will also want to take in a few of the park's historic rung-and-railing trails. "One I will recommend to people is Jordan Cliffs Trail," Sheridan continued. "It's a steep climb that brings you to the top of Penobscot Mountain; one of the ladders is cut right out of a tree. There's an iron-rung ladder as you make your way toward the top. On the cliff sides you're above tree line, and there are sweeping views of the island, including Jordan Pond below. Acadia's most famous trail is Precipice. It's short—only about a mile—but straight up 1,058 feet to the top of Champlain Mountain. The Precipice Trail has the most iron rungs and cliff exposure, and the view from the top is down on Frenchman's Bay, including the Porcupine Islands. It's great fun for me to get up on Mount Champlain and talk to other hikers as they reach the top of Precipice. Most everyone says that it was scary, but was also the greatest hike of their life—a real 'Wow!' experience. For years after, they'll bring back other friends and family members to share the experience and sense of accomplishment. One of my fondest memories of Acadia is the first time I did the Precipice Trail with my wife. Though she's an avid hiker, she's not particularly crazy about exposed walks and cliffs. Understandably, she was apprehensive about tackling Precipice, but when my daughter and son-in-law visited, she was game to try it. Like so many who make the climb, she felt a great sense of achievement in reaching the top; it's not an experience that she'll ever forget." (Note that Precipice, Jordan Cliffs, and most of the other "cliff" trails in the park are closed from spring to mid-August to protect nesting peregrine falcons.)

OPPOSITE:
From the summit of Cadillac Mountain, you can take in splendid vistas of the northern Maine coast.

It would be a shame to visit Acadia and not experience a bit of life on the smaller islands within the park's boundaries. You can visit by foot or by boat, as Sheridan explains. "There's a shorter hike that we don't always promote that takes you from Bar Harbor on Mount Desert Island out to Bar Island, then around the island. Of course, you have to do it at low tide, and make sure that you make it back to Bar Harbor in the four-hour window before the tide comes in. Kids love the idea that they've walked to an island. Another option is to take a half-day boat trip out to Baker Island, accompanied by a park ranger. The ranger points out any avian or marine mammal life encountered en route, and leads an easy-moderate hike around the island. From here, you can enjoy a great ocean view of Mount Desert Island."

For many visitors to down east Maine, the trip is not complete without at least one opportunity to tie on a bib and tuck into a fresh lobster. In 2007 (the most recent year for which statistics are available as of this writing), more than 62,000,000 pounds of lobster were harvested from Maine waters, with many coming from the cold, nutrient-rich area off Mount Desert Island. Plated, *Homarus americanus* can take infinite forms, but in these parts, locals prefer it simple—that is, steamed in its shell, with sides of melted butter and lemon. Most eateries in nearby Bar Harbor feature lobster, but you needn't stray far from the trails, as lobster is on the menu at Jordan Pond House, right in the park. "The original Jordan Pond House goes back more than 100 years," Sheridan said. "The present restaurant is set up as a teahouse, right on the shores of Jordan Pond. There's a big lawn in front of the house rolling down to the pond, and people can eat outside at picnic tables. Jordan Pond House is known for its popovers, which are served with strawberry jam and butter. A nice plus is that you can hike in any number of directions from the restaurant or make it the end of your walk."

How's that for positive reinforcement?

SHERIDAN STEELE is superintendent of Acadia National Park, a post he's held since May 2003. He has worked in the National Park Service for over thirty years and has held management positions at Rocky Mountain National Park (assistant superintendent), Black Canyon of the Gunnison National Park (superintendent), Curecanti National Recreation Area (superintendent), Fort Scott National Historic Site (superintendent), and Cuyahoga Valley National Recreation Area (management assistant). Sheridan has extensive experience dealing with public- and private-land issues related to national parks,

DESTINATION 21

including the partnering with a variety of nonprofit and local community organizations to accomplish the National Park Service mission, which is to preserve nationally significant resources while promoting their use and enjoyment. He has a BS in business administration with a minor in public relations and an MS in resources management from Ohio State University.

If You Go

▶ **Getting There:** Acadia is approximately 150 miles north of Portland, Maine, which is served by many major carriers, including Continental, Delta, and United Airlines. It's about fifty miles from Bangor, which is served by American, Continental, and Delta.

▶ **Best Time to Visit:** July and August are major tourist times and offer fairly consistent weather. June and September can also be excellent times to visit.

▶ **Accommodations:** There are several campgrounds in Acadia. Nearby Bar Harbor offers many lodging options. The Maine Office of Tourism (888-624-6345; www.visit maine.com) has a comprehensive list.

21

DESTINATION

BAXTER STATE PARK

RECOMMENDED BY **Bob Peixotto**

Each time Bob Peixotto reaches the shoulders of Mount Katahdin, he looks out on the vast tracts of wilderness and wonders, How could someone buy this?

"I've hiked all over the Northeast," Bob said, "and for me, Baxter State Park and Mount Katahdin stand apart in terms of their ruggedness and the wildness of its territory. That it exists in a forever-wild state thanks to the vision and investment of one man makes it all that much more remarkable."

Baxter State Park occupies a 209,501-acre swath of north-central Maine. Once the domain of the Wabanaki tribe, moose, and the Great Northern Paper Company, the region's mountains, lakes, and possibilities for nature-loving first came to the attention of Percival Baxter in 1903 during a fishing trip. Baxter, a scion of a wealthy Portland, Maine, family, was taken with the area's beauty and utter wildness, and as his political influence waxed, so did his efforts to have the area preserved as a park. His sentiments were eloquently expressed in a speech from 1921, during his tenure as Maine's governor:

> Maine is famous for its twenty-five hundred miles of seacoast, with its countless islands; for its myriad lakes and ponds; and for its forests and rivers. But Mount Katahdin Park will be the state's crowning glory, a worthy memorial to commemorate the end of the first and the beginning of the second century of Maine's statehood. This park will prove a blessing to those who follow us, and they will see that we built for them more wisely than our forefathers did for us.

The legislature was not swayed, but Baxter would not be deterred. His opportunity came with the stock-market crash of 1929. In 1930, the cash-poor Great Northern Paper Company agreed to sell Baxter the 6,000 acres of land that included Mount Katahdin for

OPPOSITE:
Hikers make their way along Knife's Edge, the favored approach to the summit of Mount Katahdin.

DESTINATION 22

$25,000. Baxter, in turn, deeded this land to the State of Maine, with the proviso that the land "shall forever be used for public park and recreational purposes, shall be forever left in the natural wild state, shall forever be kept as a sanctuary for wild beasts and birds, that no road or ways for motor vehicles shall hereafter ever be constructed thereon or therein."

Baxter's assertion that Katahdin would one day be viewed as the state of Maine's crowning glory received a most powerful endorsement a few years back when the L.L. Bean Company adopted the mountain as part of its logo.

There are nearly 200 miles of trails in Baxter State Park, and forty-six mountain peaks and ridges in the park's boundaries; eighteen peaks exceed 3,000 feet. But for infrequent visitors and regulars alike, a visit to Baxter State Park means an ascent of Mount Katahdin, a 5,267-foot monolith of pink and white granite, and Maine's highest point.

There are several ways to get to the crest of Katahdin; Bob described his favorite route. "I park my car at Roaring Brook Campground, and make the short hike up to the Chimney Pond Campground and spend the night. (The Baxter State Park Authority, which governs the park, limits the number of people who can make the hike each day. By going up to Chimney Pond the afternoon before, you can get a head start on the crowd.) Chimney Pond has 1,000-foot granite walls on three sides; on a clear night, the walls are bathed in moonlight. You're usually not alone at Chimney Pond, as there are other hikers who want to reach the peak as the sun is coming up.

"I like to get up as early as I can, don a headlamp and hit the trail, which takes you all around the cirque of Katahdin. I like to take the Dudley Trail to Pamola Peak, and then head across one of Katahdin's signature stretches—a ridgeline called Knife Edge. It's only four feet wide in places, and the drop is hundreds of feet in either direction. From there, it's on up to Baxter Peak. You can see forever from here, and it's all wilderness. If you make it up in the early morning, it's a magical feeling to watch the world come to life."

Baxter Peak is the northern terminus of the Appalachian Trail (AT), and Bob has been present on several occasions when backpackers have completed their epic journeys. "I watched one guy coming up along the AT at a pretty good clip. When he reached the sign indicating trail's end, he took hold of the sign and gave it a big hug. Of course we took a number of ceremonial photos for him. Another fellow finishing the trail approached us and said, 'I've been hiking this trail for so long. How do you folks feel about nudity?' He just wanted take his clothes off to celebrate his conquest of the trail."

After your climb of Katahdin is completed, you'll want to take a few days to relax and take in the tranquility of Baxter State Park's north-woods setting. The park's many lakes—including Kidney, Daicey, Grassy, and Rocky Ponds—provide excellent fishing for brook trout, one of the region's endemic species . . . and fine canoeing for those who can't be bothered to cast. Midsummer visitors can gather and gorge on wild blueberries, blackberries, and raspberries. And if you didn't happen to come upon Mr. or Mrs. Moose on the trail, you have an excellent chance of finding Maine's totem mammal at Sandy Stream Pond. "Coming upon a moose feeding in a pond all by yourself is about as close as you can get to a true wilderness experience in New England," Bob opined.

"There's a plaque at the top of Katahdin that bears a wonderful quote from Percival Baxter," he added. "It goes, 'Man is born to die. His works are short-lived. Buildings crumble, monuments decay, and wealth vanishes, but Katahdin in all its glory forever shall remain the mountain of the people of Maine.'

"When my kids were old enough to read, I encouraged them to memorize this quote. That's how much Katahdin means to me."

BOB PEIXOTTO is Chief Operations Officer at L.L. Bean in Freeport, Maine. His hobby has long been hiking in the mountains of the Northeastern U.S., with his wife and three (now grown) children. During the winter months, Bob is an avid skier, both alpine and cross-country. He is Board Chairman of Maine Huts & Trails, a nonprofit, which is creating a 180 mile trail and hut system for people-powered recreation in western Maine.

If You Go

▶ **Getting There:** Baxter State Park is approximately 160 miles north of Portland, Maine, which is served by many major carriers. It's about sixty miles from Bangor, which is served by American, Continental, and Delta.

▶ **Best Time to Visit:** The trails leading to the summit of Katahdin are open from June through October.

▶ **Accommodations:** There are ten campgrounds in Baxter State Park (www.baxterstateparkauthority.com). Reservations are required. The Katahdin Area Chamber of Commerce (www.katahdinmaine.com) lists lodging options in the region.

EL TRIUNFO BIOSPHERE RESERVE

RECOMMENDED BY **Mark Willuhn**

"For me, the trip to El Triunfo is both spiritually and physically cleansing," said Mark Willuhn, who first visited El Triunfo in 1993. "From the wonderful campesino cuisine and culture to the spectacular sense of place one gets in the cloud forest to the exhilarating exercise, my trips to El Triunfo leave me ready to take on the world again. There are so few places left where biodiversity is so strong it seems to ooze out of everything. El Triunfo is such a place."

El Triunfo is a 300,000-acre reserve that rests in the Sierra Madre mountains of southern Chiapas in Mexico. The lower-elevation regions of the reserve are a mosaic of tropical lowland forest and the upper reaches (which have altitudes exceeding 7,500 feet) comprise one of the most pristine and biologically diverse cloud forests in Mesoamerica, made up of evergreen trees and giant ferns that rise from dense forest-floor vegetation; in some places, branches may be festooned with hanging orchids. They are not perpetually cloaked in clouds, though mist will tend to appear most afternoons. "Being in the cloud forest is like walking in a dreamscape," Mark continued. "You can't necessarily see more than four or five feet. You come to a point when you're walking in this all-white world and feel you're isolated, though you're with a group. You might get this experience in other cloud forests, but on the western slope of El Triunfo, it's especially surreal."

The cloud forest habitat at El Triunfo, combined with its geographic position between the Nearctic and Neotropical biogeographical regions, has made it a rich haven for fauna of all types. Spider monkey, tapir, red brocket deer, and tayra (a Mesoamerican member of the weasel family) are regularly observed; signs of jaguar and other cat species are often seen, though sightings of the big cats are rare. There are more than sixty species of reptiles, 1,500 species of butterflies during peak migration, and somewhere in the

OPPOSITE: El Triunfo boasts one of Mesoamerica's most pristine cloud forests.

vicinity of 400 avian species, including resplendent quetzal, long-tailed manakin, and the azure-rumped tanager, one of the rarest members of the tanager family.

El Triunfo has been carefully managed to both protect its biodiversity and generate income for the local communities through ecotourism initiatives. A nonprofit entity, EcoBiosfera El Triunfo S.C., oversees El Triunfo's Ecotourism Program and limits the number of visitors to the reserve at a given time. Ecotourism trips, though hosted by different companies, follow an itinerary similar to the one Mark shares here.

"It's an adventure to get there. You drive south on paved roads from the Chiapas city of Tuxtla Gutiérrez to a dirt road that leads in the direction of El Triunfo. From here, you get in the back of a coffee truck—coffee beans are an important crop in the area—or a four-wheel-drive vehicle and ride several hours to Finca Prussia, a little settlement where the road ends. Now the hike begins. You start in shade coffee plants, and make your way up 2,500 feet through pine and oak forests that transition into cloud forest and the main camp for El Triunfo. While it's a good elevation gain, it comes via nine miles, and a well-maintained trail with lots of switchbacks makes it manageable. Plus, there are burros to carry your gear. The base camp is in an open meadow, surrounded by thick cloud forest. The first time I hiked into the camp was at night, and I was blown away at the brightness of the stars. I've never seen stars that seemed so close. The camp itself is very comfortable, with a little dorm structure and hot water. We hike up with local people, and the thing guests enjoy most is the interaction with the cooks and park rangers, who've lived around here all of their lives.

"Generally, we're at this camp three or four nights. There's a great trail system from here, all in the cloud forest environment. The Bandera Trail takes you up to Cerro Bandera, a climb of about 1,000 feet. Along the way, there's a small 'forest' of terrestrial bromeliad, and you'll sometimes meet tapir along the trail. Cerro El Triunfo is short and sweet, less than a mile. There's some hands-and-knees scrambling, but at the top you get spectacular views of base camp and the surroundings. The Palo Gordo Trail is perhaps the most strenuous of the walks, as you drop nearly 2,000 feet over the course of five miles and then must return. You have an excellent chance to see horned guan (a seldom-seen species of tree-dwelling turkey); spider monkeys have also been encountered here.

"On the last phase of the trek, we hike over the Continental Divide; on a clear day, you can see the Pacific. There's cloud-forest habitat, then cypress-dominated forest as we descend to a more primitive camp at Cañada Honda. The next day, we move through middle and lower montane tropical forest to our camp at Limonar. The last day brings us down to La Encrucijada Biosphere Reserve on the Pacific Coast. We take a boat to a research station on the preserve, and spend a few nights there, on the banks of the Huixtla River. You wiggle your toes in the mud along the shoreline. When you feel something, you wiggle it up—and it's a pottery shard from pre-Classic Mayan era.

"In the course of a week at El Triunfo, you see an entire watershed, cross the Continental Divide, and see some very special animals. It's really a spectacular thing."

MARK WILLUHN is the founder of Emerald Planet (www.emeraldplanet.com), which designs, plans, and carries out conservation-based tours with the goal of generating revenue for protected areas and conservation organizations. He has fifteen years' conservation experience, including extensive work developing sustainable-tourism programs and leading tours in Southern Mexico, Belize, Honduras, Guatemala, Nicaragua, and El Salvador. Currently, Mark manages the Mesoamerican Ecotourism Alliance, which is an innovative business model that builds local capacity; links small-scale ecotourism programs to local, regional, and international markets; and maximizes conservation benefits to protected areas in the region. Before founding Emerald Planet in 1995, Mark held positions as trips coordinator/development associate with the Nature Conservancy, and as advancement officer with the Sierra Club. Mark is affiliated with the Center for Protected Area Management and Training at Colorado State University. He holds an undergraduate degree in forestry from Colorado State University and an MBA from San Francisco State University.

If You Go

▶ **Getting There:** Trips to El Triunfo begin from Tuxtla Gutiérrez, which is served via Mexico City by Mexicana Airlines (800-380-8781; www.mexicana.com).

▶ **Best Time to Visit:** January through April are most popular.

▶ **Guides/Outfitters:** You'll need to travel with a tour company to visit El Triunfo, as access is limited to protect this biosphere. MesoAmerican Travel Alliance (800-682-0584; www.travelwithmea.org) leads trips to the region.

THE ROCKY MOUNTAIN FRONT

RECOMMENDED BY **M. A. Sanjayan**

"When you ask, 'Who are the greatest hikers in American history?,'" M. A. Sanjayan began, "Meriwether Lewis and William Clark have to be at the top of the list. If they were to return to this world and do their hike again, there's only one place they'd visit where they'd see the same plants and animals, and find the terrain little changed—the Rocky Mountain Front and Crown of the Continent. Today, you can hike in their footsteps and see the same things that they saw."

Montana's Rocky Mountain Front is a place of awesome contrasts, a majestic convergence of the Northern Rockies and Great Plains that creates one of the richest ecosystems in the Lower Forty-eight. The Nature Conservancy defines the Front as a three-hundred-by-fifty-mile swath from northern Montana through southern Alberta, Canada. This transition area of foothills makes an ideal habitat for many megacharismatic mammal species of the West—elk, moose, black bear, wolves, cougars, lynx, and wolverine—the same animals that Lewis and Clark encountered. The region also acts as a wintering range for higher-elevation animals like mountain goat and bighorn sheep, which migrate here from other sections of the vast Crown of the Continent ecosystem, which includes the Flathead River watershed, Glacier and Waterton Lakes National Parks, and large swaths of southwestern Alberta and southeastern British Columbia. It is also the last dominion of the plains grizzly bear.

When people think of grizzly-bear habitat, most picture high-mountain meadows in the northern Rockies or forlorn Alaska coastlines. But that was not always the case. Not so long ago, grizzlies wandered as far south as the Mexican border and eastward to the Great Plains of eastern Montana, North and South Dakota, Nebraska, and Kansas. In the spring of 1805, when the Corps of Discovery left their winter camp in present-day

North Dakota, they were warned by the Mandan people of the fearsome predators that awaited them to the west. Little could have properly prepared them. On May 14, Captain Lewis described one of the Corps' early encounters with a grizzly:

> About 4 in the afternoon we passed another small river on the South side, near the mouth of which some of the men discovered a large brown bear, and six of them went out to kill it. They fired at it, but having only wounded it, it made battle; the two who had reserved their fire discharged their pieces at him as he came towards them; this however only retarded his motion for a moment. The men, unable to reload their guns, took to flight, the bear pursued and had very nearly overtaken them before they reached the river. Two of the party betook themselves to a canoe and the others separated and concealed themselves among the willows, reloaded their pieces; they struck him several times again but the guns served only to direct the bear to them. In this manner he pursued two of them separately so close that they were obliged to throw aside their guns and pouches and throw themselves into the river, although the bank was nearly 20 feet perpendicular. So enraged was this animal that he plunged into the river only a few feet behind the second man he had compelled to take refuge in the water, when one of those who still remained on shore shot him through the head and finally killed him.

This encounter was solidly in the plains of what is now Garfield County, Montana, some 200 miles east of the Rockies.

Biologists believe that nearly 100,000 grizzlies once ranged from the Rockies through the Great Plains. In their eastern reaches, they relied heavily on the vast buffalo herds as a food source. Due to the decimation of the buffalo and relentless hunting by frightened settlers, the grizzly were eliminated from most of their original range; those that remained were driven to the mountains, far from human encroachment.

There are countless places where hikers can access the varied topography along the Rocky Mountain Front and have a chance to come upon a plains grizzly. Sanjayan likes using Pine Butte Swamp Preserve as a base. "The Nature Conservancy has a property there, Pine Butte Guest Ranch, which is convenient to many hikes that take you into a very real wilderness—and home at night to a warm shower and a soft bed." The Pine Butte Swamp Preserve is the largest wetland complex along the Front, a 15,500-acre montage of foothills prairie, rocky ridges of limber pine and juniper, spruce-fir forests, mountain streams, glacial ponds, and spring-fed fen. Situated just west of the town of

Choteau, Montana and adjoining the Bob Marshall Wilderness, Pine Butte provides ideal foraging ground for grizzlies. The bears descend from their winter hibernation lairs in the mountains in the spring to replenish their energy stores among the easy pickings—berries, roots, and the like—of the swamps and prairie land. Most will return to the mountains in the summer as foraging improves there. (Hiking on the preserve itself is seasonally limited so as not to disturb the bears.)

"Much of the private land around Pine Butte (over 50,000 additional acres) has been secured for wildlife through conservation easements," Sanjayan added. "The bears need a great deal of uninterrupted open land to range upon—as much as 250 square miles for a mature male. It's the Nature Conservancy's goal to secure enough high quality bear habitat in the region to sustain the populations and maintain critical linkages between public and private lands that enable bears to continue their seasonal movements. If you visit now with your children, it should be much the same when they return with their children."

Two popular day hikes around Pine Butte are Clary Coulee and Our Lake. The former climbs a bench that offers perspectives of both the endless plains to the east and high limestone walls of the Front to the west. The transition zone that makes the region so unique is presented in stark relief. The hike to Our Lake gives you access to one of the few alpine lakes that can be reached from the eastern side of the Front. The trail meanders past several waterfalls; once you reach the lake, you're likely to see mountain goats scrambling about the talus slopes. If you pack a fishing rod along, Our Lake's cutthroat trout are eager to take a fly or spinner.

DR. M. A. SANJAYAN is lead scientist for the Nature Conservancy (TNC). He is originally from Sri Lanka, and at an early age his family moved to Africa, which is where he discovered his passion for wildlife. He completed his PhD at the University of California, Santa Cruz, where he did his thesis work on genetics and demography with Dr. Michael Soule, one of the founding fathers of the field of conservation biology. After a short stint at the World Bank, Sanjayan joined TNC in 1999, first as the director of science for the California program, and later as one of three lead scientists for the organization as a whole. He splits his time between the science office and the marketing and philanthropy department. His primary responsibility is to communicate the scientific and conservation breakthroughs that TNC is pioneering to a broad, external audience and to the group's donors and supporters. Further, he is responsible for recognizing trends and

DESTINATION **24**

OPPOSITE:
The area where
the northern
Rockies and
the Great Plains
converge provides
habitat for the
last populations
of plains grizzly
bears.

risks identified by the global scientific and conservation community and ensuring that TNC is not only aware of such trends but is able to deal with them appropriately. Sanjayan writes a monthly column, "Wild Life," for TNC; is a frequent contributor to magazine articles and radio and television shows; and is currently working on a book about poverty and conservation. He also has a faculty appointment at University of Montana, where he occasionally teaches graduate seminar classes. Sanjayan lives in Missoula, Montana, where the fishing is excellent and where all the species seen by the Lewis and Clark Expedition are still around.

If You Go

▶ **Getting There:** The closest airport to the Pine Butte Swamp Preserve and the Rocky Mountain Front is in Great Falls, Montana, which is served by Allegiant Air (702-505-8888; www.allegiantair.com), Delta (800-221-1212; www.delta.com), Horizon (800-547-9308; www.horizonair.com), and United (800-864-8331; www.united.com).

▶ **Best Time to Visit:** May through September provides the most consistent weather and best bear-viewing opportunities. Higher passes may have snow into early July. In mid-May, the Nature Conservancy hosts the "Path of the Great Bear" workshop at Pine Butte, with noted grizzly expert Dr. Charles Jonkel.

▶ **Accommodations:** The Pine Butte Guest Ranch (406-466-2158; www.pinebutteguestranch.com) is an ideal base camp for exploration of the Rocky Mountain Front. Several motor lodges are also available in Choteau, including the Stage Stop Inn (888-466-5900; www.stagestopinn.com).

DESTINATION 24

GLACIER NATIONAL PARK

RECOMMENDED BY **Randy Gayner**

Lacking geysers, bison, and fumaroles, Glacier National Park is perhaps destined to forever be Montana's *second*-favorite national park. But hikers—day-trippers and back-country enthusiasts alike—have long appreciated Glacier's 700 miles of hiking trails, and the abundant opportunities for transcendence and isolation they afford.

"I had visited many of the national parks in the western United States with my parents as I was growing up," Randy Gayner recalled, "and the mountains of Glacier made a tremendous impression on me. When I finished college, I found a summer job there. Once I was out there, I thought it would be crazy for me to start my adult life back in Cleveland, when the Glacier area provided such a spectacular venue for outdoors folks like myself. Almost thirty years later, I'm still here."

Glacier National Park comprises more than one million acres in northwestern Montana; the park abuts the Canadian provinces of Alberta and British Columbia, and is contiguous with Canada's Waterton Lakes National Park. Contrary to popular perception, the park is named not for existing glaciers (of which a few do remain), but for the work earlier glaciers did at the conclusion of the last ice age. These glaciers slowly scoured away deep valleys and sharp ridges, carving rugged mountains and deep lakes en route. "The most special thing for me about Glacier is the tremendous amount of high alpine country you find here," Randy continued. "Since we're so far north, a lot of our high country is above tree line. Our mountains are actually a southern extension of the Canadian Rockies, more sedimentary in composition than the granitic American Rockies. The way these formations have worn away adds to their dramatic nature. Glacier is also special because of its abundant animal life. Every big-game animal that was here originally is still here—wolf, mountain lion, wolverine, lynx . . . and, of course, grizzly bear.

113

The presence of these predators, especially the bears, intensifies your senses. It gives any hiking experience here a little extra pizzazz."

Some two million visitors come to take in Glacier each year, though many of those folks do not range much beyond the Going-to-the-Sun Road, which cuts across the center of the park from west to east. The fifty-two-mile highway is frequently ranked as one of the most beautiful roads in the world, and many of the park's trademark characteristics—from glacial lakes to windswept passes—are visible from its macadam. As it turns out, the Going-to-the-Sun Road is also the launching point for one of Glacier's most noteworthy day hikes, the Highline Trail. "The trail begins at Logan Pass, the high point of Going-to-the-Sun [at 6,646 feet]," Randy described, "and parallels the Continental Divide for seven miles. The hike is all above tree line, providing for wide-open, grand vistas." The high vantage point, unbroken by trees, makes the Highline an excellent wildlife-viewing trail. "You almost always see mountain goats and bighorn sheep," Randy continued. "The animals are used to seeing people and don't spook easily, so photographers can get some great shots. The Highline is also a good trail to see grizzlies—at a comfortable distance! There's a valley down below that we've nicknamed Bear Valley, for the many times we've watched bears from above." The Highline has other things going for it: It's one of Glacier's least punishing trails, with many extended flat sections, and at the end of the trail the Granite Park Chalet awaits, with snacks and beverages available.

Another of Randy's favorite day hikes is the trail to Iceberg Lake. "Iceberg Lake is in the Many Glacier Valley in the northeastern section of the park. The valley is a great place to base yourself, as there are many wonderful day hikes from here." The Iceberg Lake trail unfolds through open terrain, framed by Mount Wilbur in the background and the Ptarmigan Wall to the west, which towers nearly 3,000 feet above the trail. Like Highline, Iceberg Lake is one of the gentler walks in Glacier, gaining a modest 1,200 feet in elevation over four and a half miles. It's also a productive trail for finding grizzlies. These characteristics, and its astounding scenery, make it another visitor favorite. "Iceberg Lake itself is tucked back into a cirque, in the shadows of Mount Wilbur," Randy explained. "It doesn't get a lot of sun, especially against the north wall. Snow holds in there for a long time, but as the summer goes on, large chunks of snow and ice will calve off. There are usually small icebergs floating around on the lake, hence the name."

With a million acres to explore, Glacier offers no shortage of backcountry hiking opportunities, where you're sure to leave the crowds behind. Randy shared a few of his

*OPPOSITE:
Following the
Continental
Divide above
treeline, the High
Line Trail offers
long views and
the chance to
glimpse mountain
goats, bighorn
and grizzly.*

DESTINATION

25

favorites. "For a shorter backpacking trip—say, three days—I love the Dawson–Pitamakan Pass hike in the Two Medicine region of the park. It's about twenty miles, so you don't need to cover too much ground each day. The campgrounds on Old Man Lake and No Name Lake are spectacular, and between Dawson Pass and Pitamakan, you walk a ridge-line along the Continental Divide. There are huge views to the east and the west—and enough wind to blow you off your feet! This was a sacred area for the Blackfeet Indians. They called it the Backbone of the World. For a longer backpacking trip, the Boulder Pass–Brown Pass trail in the north of the park is a favorite. In the section between Brown and Boulder Pass, you spend several days up in high alpine country, with huge wildflower meadows. The most spectacular place to camp in Glacier is just off the trail near Boulder Pass, a spot called Hole in the Wall. It's a cirque with waterfalls all around, and a little creek that runs through the middle of the campsite."

RANDY GAYNER came to Montana after finishing college, and he never left. After first working as a backcountry ranger based out of the Polebridge Ranger district in Glacier National Park, Randy founded Glacier Guides and Montana Raft Company in 1983. When he's not holding his trusty clipboard, you can find him floating local rivers, ski patrolling up on Big Mountain, or scouting for another fun adventure.

If You Go

▶ **Getting There:** Visitors can fly to Kalispell, Montana, which is served by Alaska Airlines (800-252-7522; www.alaskaair.com) and United (800-864-8331; www.united.com).
▶ **Best Time to Visit:** Peak hiking season is June through September. The Glacier National Park Web site (www.nps.gov/glac) lists trail conditions.
▶ **Accommodations:** In addition to many campgrounds, there are a number of lodging options inside Glacier National Park; all are highlighted on the park's Web site (www.nps .gov/glac). The Flathead Convention & Visitor Bureau (800-543-3105; www.fcvb.org) highlights lodging outside the park.
▶ **Guides/Outfitters:** Glacier Guides and Montana Raft Company (800-521-7238; www .glacierguides.com) leads both day and backcountry hikes in Glacier National Park.

THE HIGH ATLAS

RECOMMENDED BY **Mark Gordon**

Resting at the fulcrum of Europe and northern Africa, Morocco is a colorful land that has long enticed adventurous travelers. It's a place where snow-capped mountains rise from the edges of an inhospitable desert, where millennium-old neighborhoods survive in the midst of modern cityscapes. "I made my first trip to Morocco as a Peace Corps volunteer," Mark Gordon recalled, "and decided pretty quickly that I wanted to stay. I was taken with the country's tremendously varied topography. I was also attracted by the warmth of the people, especially in the high mountains—people known by some as the Berbers.

"For trekkers, Morocco—and more specifically, the High Atlas—has several appeals. One of the charms is that the chain has two massifs above 4,000 meters (13,123 feet)—a mythic height for Europeans. Another is the chance to have a glimpse of the Berber way of life. Some of the valleys we trek through are extremely remote, accessible only on foot, and only for six months of the year. People in these valleys live very much as they did 200 years ago, with the exception that they may have Coca Cola and soap that's brought in on mules . . . the pick-up truck of the High Atlas." (Mark pointed out that the term many Moroccan people use to describe themselves is *Amazigh*; the term "Berber" is a bastardization of the name the Romans gave these people, "Barbar," or "barbarian." The Amazigh are considered the indigenous inhabitants of northern Africa.)

The High Atlas runs across central Morocco, from near the Atlantic in the west to the border with Algeria in the east; it's part of the larger Atlas Mountain Range, which spreads across the top of northern Africa for 1,500 miles across Morocco, Algeria, and Tunisia. The region where Mark leads many treks is near the center of the High Atlas, in the vicinity of Mount M'Goun, North Africa's second-highest peak, at 13,343 feet. Here, craggy limestone peaks and sheer red-rock canyons adjoin rushing streams and green pastures.

The trek begins in the Aït Bougmez valley and proceeds south toward the M'Goun massif, passing picturesque mud-brick villages where women in brightly hued dresses (made of hand-dyed yarns) tend fields of wheat, barley, potatoes, and clover. The men of the villages spend much of the summer higher in the mountains, grazing their sheep and cultivating crops on small plots of land near the river. On the second day of the trek, you'll reach the top of Oumskiyq Pass, at more than 10,000 feet, where you're afforded breathtaking vistas of Mount M'Goun. This is an excellent primer for the optional hike to the summit of M'Goun the following day.

"Though it's a fairly long day of walking, I love the summit route," Mark continued. "It's what I'd call a trekker's peak, hard but straightforward and nontechnical—not unlike Kilimanjaro. Before the summit, there's a ridge that's a mile long. It can be as wide as a driveway, or as narrow as a sidewalk, and you're 13,000 feet up. It's spectacular." Those who opt for the lower route will come upon a startling sight—a herd of camels grazing in an alpine valley. "There are nomadic Amazigh who engage in the tradition of transhumance—a practice where herders move their animals long distances according to grazing seasons. These Amazigh winter their animals in the Sahara desert and bring them up to the High Atlas in the summer."

Trekkers are sometimes treated to encounters with the camels' owners. "We can't be sure of an encounter with these herdsmen, but they do often camp along our hiking route," Mark explained. "If we come upon them, they'll inevitably invite us to join them for tea. There's a long tradition of hospitality among these people, and it's customary to offer travelers food and drink. On one occasion, a group I was trekking with was invited to attend a nomad wedding. There were more than a hundred herdsmen and their families gathered. There's lots of singing and dancing at these weddings, and we were present for a few songs. Musicians have percussion instruments that resemble large tambourines, and one player might have a crude violin; the body of the instrument might be a two-gallon oil can, the neck a broom handle or carved tree branch, the strings steel or fishing line. The men and women form in different lines and sing in a call-and-response fashion. One song can go on for half an hour."

From the shadow of Mount M'Goun, the trail angles toward Oulilimt Valley, one of the most remote of the populated valleys of the High Atlas. In the valley, you'll have a chance to visit some the residents of the village of Im Nict. "The people of Im Nict live very much like their ancestors, due to their isolation," Mark said. We have mint tea with a family, and

OPPOSITE:
The rugged High Atlas Mountains of Morocco are home to isolated populations of Amazigh people (sometimes called Berbers).

DESTINATION

26

119

get to see their home and how they live." Leaving Oulilimt Valley, the trek follows gorges formed by the M'Goun River—in fact, much of the day is spent crossing back and forth across the river. Though a bit hard on the ankles, the gorges are inspiring—at some places, just ten feet across and over 4,000 feet tall.

Once your trek of the central High Atlas is complete, you may wish to trade the quiet solitude of the canyon country for the colorful maelstrom that is Marrakech. "It's a lovely city, very lush," Mark described. "For size, variety, and density, the souk here is incredible. And though it's no secret, you simply can't leave Marrakech without visiting the Djemma el Fna. It's a swirling, 365-day-a-year carnival in a square, replete with dancers, musicians, storytellers, fortunetellers, magicians, and snake charmers."

MARK GORDON is an American who fell in love with Morocco after serving in the country as a Peace Corps volunteer. He has lived in Morocco since 1982 and has led numerous expeditions and journeys throughout North Africa for Wilderness Travel. He loves the the Sahara and also has a particular affection for the High Atlas mountains and the Amazigh people who live there. Mark also guides cultural and hiking journeys in Mali. He speaks French and Moroccan Arabic, and has some knowledge of Berber dialects.

If You Go

▶ **Getting There:** High Atlas trekkers can fly into either Casablanca or Marrakech, Morocco, which are served by a number of carriers, including Air France (800-237 2747; www.airfrance.com) and Royal Air Maroc (www.royalairmaroc.com).

▶ **Best Time to Visit:** July and August are the most reliable times to trek the High Atlas.

▶ **Accommodations:** The Moroccan National Tourist office (+212 537 67 40 13; www .visitmorocco.com) lists lodging options around Morocco for before and after your trek.

▶ **Guides/Outfitters:** A number of travel companies lead treks into the High Atlas, including Wilderness Travel (800-368-2794; www.wildernesstravel.com).

THE NAUKLUFT TRAIL

RECOMMENDED BY **Kobus Alberts**

When asked what sort of walker comes to Namibia to hike the Naukluft Trail, Kobus Alberts chuckled for a moment, then said, "People who are somewhat mad! The Naukluft is a seriously tough trek. Water is very scarce, it can be quite hot, there's little support so you're required to carry a heavy pack, and there are some difficult scrambles. Its ruggedness came as a surprise for me. On my first visits here, I hiked just a few parts of the walk. It wasn't until I did the whole trail that I realized how special it was. On the Naukluft, your soul can run free."

Namibia is a large, sparsely populated nation on the southwest coast of southern Africa, bordered by Angola to the north, Botswana to the east, and South Africa to the south. It is one of the driest places on earth; in parts of the Namib Desert, which stretches nearly the entire length of the Namibian coast and covers more than 30,000 square miles of the nation, less than an inch of rain falls annually. A number of hardy plants and animals have evolved to withstand the aridity, soaking up moisture from the fog that blows in from the Atlantic. (One of the most curious of these plants is *Welwitschia mirabilis*, a low-growing shrub that can live for more than a thousand years.) Much of the desert is incorporated in the Namib-Naukluft National Park, an expansive game preserve that totals more than 19,000 square miles, making it Namibia's biggest park and one of the largest parks in Africa. In addition to hosting some of the world's tallest sand dunes, which can top one thousand feet, the easternmost section of the park takes in the Naukluft Mountains, which were initially set aside as protected habitat for the threatened Hartmann's mountain zebra. (The zebra preserve was rolled into Namib Desert Park to create the current national park.) The Nauklufts reach heights approaching 6,000 feet, and are peppered with abundant kopjes—Afrikaans for rock outcroppings. In addition to

121

the zebra, the park is home to kudu, klipspringer, baboon, and leopard, as well as more than 200 bird species.

It's in this mountainous section of the park where the Naukluft Trail unfolds. It's seventy-two miles are generally hiked over eight days. (The very fit—or, to paraphrase Kobus's words, the extremely crazy—can shave the hike to seven days. Anyone who wishes to hike Naukluft must submit a physical exam from their doctor forty days prior to their departure, attesting to their fitness.) Stopping points are well defined—they're not exactly huts or lodges, but shelters built from stone block, divided into four compartments, with a corrugated roof, basic toilet facilities, and a water pump. Refuse bins are available at four of the shelters to help you lighten your load. Crowding is seldom a concern on the Naukluft; in fact, it would be uncommon to see anyone outside of your party once you embark on the trail. Within a few minutes of leaving the Naukluft Hut (where many walkers choose to stay the night before starting their hike), the appeals of the place become apparent. "You begin in a kind of gorge, then climb a small hill. You contour along the side of the hill with a massive drop to the side, and then come out on a plateau," Kobus described, "and you're struck with majestic views—mountains and plains as far as you can see. It's a very dramatic opening."

Midway through the following day, hikers descend into spectacular Ubisis Kloof (Afrikaans for gorge). Several sets of chains assist with a fairly precipitous descent, in part down a dry waterfall. The kloofs, cut into granite throughout the Naukluft Mountains, hold just enough water to sustain life for its denizens. A pleasant surprise awaits at the bottom of Ubisis after a stroll up a dry riverbed—instead of a rock shelter, hikers sleep in a former holiday cottage, complete with bunk beds, mattresses, and a shower . . . that is, if the pump is working. "I hiked into Ubisis on one occasion, and there was no water in the tank," Kobus recalled. "Some baboons had broken the pump, which happens occasionally here, as all living creatures are constantly in quest of water. As I worked on the pump, a black mamba suddenly appeared. I was in awe of this creature, a sleek, mean fighting machine." (The black mamba is one of the world's most venomous and feared snakes, averaging eight feet in length. The snake's body is not black but dark olive; the name comes from the dark shade of the mamba's mouth.)

After ascending Ubisis Kloof, the third day on Naukluft provides a bit of relief, as it's mostly level along a plateau and, at seven miles, it's fairly short. Hartmann's mountain zebra are often encountered on this portion of the trek. The zebras live in family groups,

OPPOSITE:
The Naukluft
Trail cuts across
the Namib
Desert, one of
the driest places
on earth.

DESTINATION

27

generally of five to ten animals, rather than in the large herds favored by plains zebras. They seem able to smell moisture, and have been observed digging in river beds to get to water. "I'm always excited to come upon a mountain zebra," Kobus added. "They're such agile animals despite their stocky size. You won't believe the terrain that these large animals can traverse. The protection plan has been very successful, as populations in Naukluft are now believed to be above 25,000." Day four brings visitors into the Tsams River Gorge, passing a number of delightful springs, oases within this austere landscape. With previous planning, it's possible to depart the trail here, though the truly challenging walking lies ahead.

Day six may be the most grueling segment of the Naukluft, but it may also be the most rewarding. After a 650-foot climb to the top of a waterfall—again, abetted by chains—the trail enters a gorge, climbing some 2,000 feet. It's a grueling walk with large boulders that must be periodically scaled, but hikers are treated to a special sight en route—rock formations called tufa, a sedimentary rock with a heavy concentration of carbonates. "One of the tufa formations is nearly 500 feet high," Kobus said. "It resembles a waterfall that has frozen." The next day, the trail scales Bakenskop, the tallest point on the Naukluft at 6,400 feet. The day's walk begins by entering the Arbeid Adelt Kloof, and gets progressively more strenuous until the trail reaches a dry waterfall. "From here, you have to climb eighty feet, almost straight up, with the help of a chain," Kobus continued. "When you reach the top of the kloof, you're 2,000 feet above the Tsondab Valley. The very top of Bakenskop is called World's View, and it's not an overstatement. You can see forever and ever across the plains."

KOBUS ALBERTS is a native Namibian and has spent more than ten years living in the national parks and game reserves of his country. Most recently, he's been heading up the National Marine Aquarium of Namibia in the city of Swakopmund. Kobus is a senior instructor for Expedition Medicine's desert-medicine course (for medical professionals) and a key member of the Namibia ultramarathon team. He has participated in expeditions to Greenland and Antarctica. Kobus is founding director of Wild at Heart Safaris, a Namibian-owned and -based safari company that specializes in adventure and luxury safari tours for small groups and families.

DESTINATION

27

If You Go

▶ **Getting There:** International travelers generally enter Namibia via the capital, Windhoek, which is served from Europe by Air Namibia (+264-61-299-6111; www.airnamibia.com.na), and from South Africa by British Airways (800-247-9297; www.britishairways.com) and South African Airways (800-722-9675; www.flysaa.com).

▶ **Best Time to Visit:** The trail is open to hikers from March 1 to October 31; conditions are too warm in the austral summer for hiking.

▶ **Guides/Outfitters:** Wild at Heart Safaris (+264-81-122-9342; www.wildatheartsafaris.com) leads adventures on the Naukluft Trail.

DESTINATION

27

ANNAPURNA SANCTUARY

RECOMMENDED BY **Duncan Baker**

"I first went to Nepal in 1979," Duncan Baker began, "as I was serving in the British Army, and was dispatched to work with the Gurkhas [a brigade of Nepalese soldiers who have fought for Great Britain since the early 1800s]. I found myself trekking all over the Annapurnas and western Nepal, as the men we recruited came from that region. My long treks piqued my interest in the country and its people. After my stint in the army was finished, I eventually made my way back to the Annapurnas with a view to starting a trekking company that could employ some of my retired Gurkha comrades."

"Trekking" and "Nepal"—the two words go together like "bread and butter" or "Lennon and McCartney." With a northern border that straddles the Himalaya Mountains for its entire length, Nepal has long had the terrain to titillate and astound walkers. The conceptual framework for making Nepal a trekking center can be traced to Colonel Jimmy Roberts, a former Gurkha officer and military attaché at the British Embassy in Kathmandu. Well familiar with Nepal's mountains and valleys, Colonel Roberts had the notion to provide visitors with tents and local guides—Sherpas—to lead them through the countryside and prepare meals. (While the term "Sherpa" has come to mean mountain guide or porter for many, Sherpas are actually an ethnic group from Tibet who have lived in Nepal for more than 300 years.) This was in 1965. The next year, less than a hundred trekker-tourists visited Nepal. In 2002, it was estimated that some 70,000 visitors engaged in some level of Nepalese hiking. The treks are broken into two broad categories: full trekking, where you (and your porters) carry your gear and make and break a tent camp each night, as on a backpacking trip; and teahouse trekking, where you stay in a lodge as you follow the route, rather like hut hiking in the Alps or New Zealand.

OPPOSITE: Machhapuchhre (or Fish Tail Mountain) towers above Annapurna.

DESTINATION

28

The first trek that comes to mind for many would-be Nepal trekkers is the expedition to the base camp at Everest—after all, who hasn't thought about at least getting close to the world's tallest mountain? "When people come to us with an interest in hiking to Everest Base Camp, we're happy to oblige them," Duncan continued. "But we try to be clear about what's involved. It's a considerable time commitment, and the altitudes encountered on that walk (more than 18,000 feet) make some people think twice. I like to present Annapurna as a great alternative. You can get into the mountains easily, starting at altitudes of 3,000 feet. You have a host of incredible mountains right in front of you. You can go as high as you wish—up to 13,550 feet. And on a trek like the Annapurna Sanctuary, can get a great taste of the Nepalese hiking experience, whether you're only able to spare two days for a trek or have two weeks."

The Annapurna Sanctuary is a high glacial basin that rests between the city of Pokhara to the south and the mountains to the north. "It's not called a 'sanctuary' because of laws that protect wildlife within its boundaries," Duncan explained, "but because of its natural serenity, beauty, and the local belief of the divine presence of the Hindu goddesses Annapurna and Gangapurna. Sitting in Sanctuary Meadows at 13,200 feet, surrounded by a 360-degree panorama of incredible Himalayan peaks—Hiunchuli, Annapurna South, Fang, Annapurna II, Roc Noir, Glacier Dome, Gangapurna, Annapurna III, and Machhapuchhre—towering nearly two miles above you, is a sublime experience. And it can only be reached on one trail."

The Annapurna Sanctuary trek begins in Lumle, an hour north of Pokhara. At the outset, you're at a modest elevation of 3,000 feet, in the shadow of Machhapuchhre (22,943 feet), sometimes called Fish Tail Mountain, an abrupt spire that's been likened to the Matterhorn. Over the next six days, you gradually gain altitude as you make your way toward Panchenin Barha, a narrow point in the canyon that serves as a natural "gate" to the sanctuary; Annapurna Base Camp lies just a few miles ahead. "One of the aspects I like about this trek is that it takes you through a host of climatic zones—subtropical, temperate, and alpine," Duncan said. "You also pass through a number of mountain villages where the people have been doing subsistence farming for hundreds of years—growing rice in the lower elevations, corn and potatoes at higher altitudes. If you push along hard, you can make it into the base camp and out in seven days, but I like to take a few extra days so I can linger in the villages and get a sense of life there; our notion has always been that you'll see the mountains, yes, but you'll also experience village life. There are four lodges that we built along the trekking route in the 1990s that guests stay at, and several teahouses that we frequent. The idea is that you walk four or five hours each day, arrive in time for a late lunch and plenty of time to explore the villages, then have a warm shower and a soft bed."

Cultural lessons aside, the sights along the Sanctuary trail are an intoxicating attraction. On the alpine sections of the trail there are vast forests of rhododendron, and in spring bloom they paint the valleys in a riot of color, abetted by magnolia and accented with ferns and orchids. Nearly 500 birds have been identified, among them resident satyr tragopan and cheer pheasant, both threatened species. For Duncan, it's hard to beat early mornings along the trail. "Every morning, I like to be up at sunrise with a mug of hot coffee or tea. On the first few days of the trek, it's not very cold as you're not at altitude. I love to watch the local people making their way to their fields, so calm and peaceful. It's almost always clear in the early morning, and you feel the sun as it lights up the enormous mountains."

DUNCAN BAKER served as an officer in the British army with the Gurkhas, which first took him to Nepal in 1979. After leaving the army, he returned to Nepal to start a trekking company with some of his former comrades, and eventually built a number of small, comfortable lodges in the Annapurnas. He is a director of Ker & Downey Nepal and spends much of the year in Nepal.

If You Go

▶ **Getting There:** International travelers will fly into Kathmandu, Nepal, which is served by a number of carriers, including Thai Airways (800-426-5204; www.thaiair.com). From here, it's a brief flight to Pokhara, which is served by a number of domestic carriers, including Buddha Air (+ 977 1 5542494; www.buddhaair.com).

▶ **Best Time to Visit:** October and November are the most popular months to visit, as the weather is generally clear. Early spring—March and April—can also have clearer weather, as well as great rhododendron displays.

▶ **Guides/Outfitters:** Many companies sell and lead trips to Annapurna, including Ker & Downey (+977-61-523-701; www.trekking-nepal.com).

THE MILFORD TRACK

RECOMMENDED BY **Shaun Liddy**

Even the most literary members of the hiking fraternity may be hard pressed to recall the verse of Blanche Baughan, a poet and social reformer who was born in England but spent most of her adult life in New Zealand. But one line of Miss Baughan's, from a 1908 dispatch she published in the *London Spectator*, has been repeated again and again, to the point where few remember where it came from: "The finest walk in the world." (In truth, Miss Baughan called her piece "A Fine Walk"; an editor at the *London Spectator* who had never set foot in New Zealand changed the title to "The Finest Walk in the World." The story was referring to the Milford Track.

"The Milford Track has such a big reputation internationally that many people don't arrive with a clear expectation of what they're going to find," began Shaun Liddy. "They understand that it's special, but they don't know exactly why. When they complete the walk and leave Milford Sound, they generally leave with memories of a richly contrasting landscape, the special birds they've seen, and the people they've met on the trail. Some of these visitors might not do other walks in their day-to-day life. My hope is that tramping the Milford Track kick-starts them into doing more walking in the future."

The thirty-three-and-a-half-mile Milford Track slices through the heart of Fiordland National Park, a 4,864-square-mile preserve along the very southwestern coast of the South Island of New Zealand, bordering the Tasman Sea. Here, the southern reach of the rugged Southern Alps, some approaching elevations of 9,000 feet, butt against the coast, and jagged fiords cut in among the mountains. The combination of steep mountains, dark-green forest, snowcapped peaks, sheer granite canyons, foaming waterfalls, and fingers of blue fjords make Fiordland one of the most visually stunning temperate regions in the world. The track begins at the northern end of Lake Te Anau and winds in a north-

OPPOSITE:
Sandfly Point
marks the end
of the Milford
Track. From
here, it's a
short boat ride
to Milford
Sound.

DESTINATION

29

131

westerly direction to its terminus at Milford Sound—itself considered New Zealand's most renowned tourist attraction, with sheer rock faces climbing thousands of feet from the sea where penguins, seals, and dolphins frolic.

Before the New Zealand tourism officials got their hands on Miss Baughan's famous summation, the route that became known as the Milford Track was destined for visitors. In 1880, Donald Sutherland, the first European resident of Milford Sound, came upon a magnificent waterfall while hiking inland. After naming the falls in his own honor, Sutherland tried building a track from the coast so he could show off his discovery to tourists arriving by steamboat. The terrain proved too difficult, however, and soon a new route was pioneered from the northern end of Lake Te Anau. After several setbacks, this route's proponents—Quintin Mackinnon and Ernest Mitchell—found success. Mackinnon went on to be the first guide to lead intrepid guests along the track to Milford Sound, sustaining his sports in part on scones called pompolonas, made from mutton-fat candles. After completing this lengthy (and often quite wet) excursion, Mackinnon and his guests would reverse direction and walk back. (A highway connecting Milford Sound and Te Anau was completed in 1954, allowing trampers to motor back to their starting point.)

A tramp of the Milford Track ("tramp" is Kiwi parlance for a hike or trek) begins with a boat ride from Te Anau Downs harbor to the trailhead at the north end of the lake. Admission is closely regulated to control overcrowding: Independent trampers have four days and three nights to complete the trail, while those taking a guided hike have an extra day and night at their avail. All parties are incentivized to complete their tramp on time, as only two boats a day leave the walk's terminus at Sandfly Point to take you across Milford Sound . . . and, as the name implies, the little pests are thick at Sandfly Point, and only a masochist would wish to linger there. On the trail, all walkers stay in huts; those for independent trampers are a few miles beyond the guided-walkers' lodges and are provided with decent amenities—gas cookers, tables, cold running water, lighting, heating, and bunkrooms with mattresses. The private lodges have more luxuriant amenities, including hot showers, three-course meals, snug beds, washing and drying facilities, and a cash bar with beer and wine.

Your walk on the Milford Track slowly crescendos. The first five miles, you traipse through beech forests along the banks of the Clinton River, one of the South Island's many fine trout streams. (Fly anglers the world over travel here for the chance to cast tiny flies to oversize brown and rainbow trout.) The next ten miles take you up gradually toward Mackinnon Pass, passing over many streams that can be trickles or torrents, depending on the rainfall (more on that later). Soon, the terrain opens up and you'll have your first view of Mackinnon Pass and the Pompolona Ice Field. Day three is the high point for most trampers, the day you reach the pass and come upon Sutherland Falls. The track zigzags over eleven switchbacks before reaching the pass at 3,507 feet. "Looking upon the Mackinnon Memorial that's a bit below the pass, you can't help but think of the explorers who were here before you," Shaun continued. "When you come out on the top of the pass, you're hit with this view of a massive glacier and immense mountains opening up all before you. It's one of the defining points of the walk." From Mackinnon Pass, it's a few hours down to Sutherland Falls, a brief detour off the main track. "It's New Zealand's highest waterfall, over 1,900 feet high, and tumbles down in three leaps," Shaun added. "A story goes that Sutherland brought a photographer up here shortly after his discovery of the falls. The photographer was dumbstruck. Sutherland later said, "So wonderstricken were we both that the whole time we were there [two days] I do not think that twenty words passed between us.'"

If the Milford Track (and, for that matter, the west coast of the South Island) has received any negative reviews, they are for the weather. While the sun can certainly shine there, you're likely to see some rain—and perhaps a good deal of it. Shaun wouldn't have it any other way. "The Milford Track is in a temperate rainforest, and we get tremendous rainfall—we can get eight inches in a day quite easily. (Milford Sound averages in the vicinity of 250 inches of rain a year.) There are times when you're on a section of the track where it's generally dry, and a good rain can bring the water up to your knees . . . or higher. But it goes away as quickly as it comes. And the rain brings thousands of waterfalls into play that you don't experience if the weather has been dry. I believe that you haven't seen the Milford Track properly until you've seen it in the rain."

SHAUN LIDDY is the head guide for Ultimate Hikes. Born in Dunedin, New Zealand, and raised in Waikouaiti, Shaun had plenty of contact with Fiordland and Mount Aspiring national parks growing up. Since joining Ultimate Hikes, he has served as a multiday guide on the Milford Track Guided Walk and became head guide for that trail in 2006. Shaun added the Routeburn Track to his responsibilities in 2008.

If You Go

► **Getting There:** Queenstown, New Zealand, is generally the staging area for tramping the Milford Track. Air New Zealand (800-262-1234; www.airnewzealand.com) offers service to Queenstown through Air New Zealand Link via Auckland or Christchurch.

► **Best Time to Visit:** The austral spring and summer—mid-November to mid-March—provide the most reliable weather, though the season can extend a month in each direction. The New Zealand Department of Conservation regulates the number of walkers on the Milford Track, and the hike is popular in the high season, so it's important for independent walkers to book ahead of time through the Great Walks Booking Office (+64 3 249-8514; www.doc.govt.nz).

► **Accommodations:** Destination Queenstown (+64 3 441-0700; www.queenstown-nz .co.nz) lists accommodations in the region's hub town. Destination Fiordland (www.fiord land.org.nz) lists lodging options in Te Anau.

► **Guides/Outfitters:** Ultimate Hikes New Zealand (+64 3 450-1940; www.ultimate hikes.co.nz) leads guided walks on the Milford Track, billeting clients at private (and more opulent) lodging.

DESTINATION

29

THE ROUTEBURN TRACK

RECOMMENDED BY **Jemma Knowles**

Most serious walkers have heard of the Milford Track (page 131) on the South Island of New Zealand, but what of the nearby Routeburn Track? Maybe not so much. "Though in the same region, the Routeburn is quite different from the Milford Track," Jemma Knowles opined. "The Milford is mostly a valley walk, whereas much of the Routeburn is along the tops of mountains. On the Milford, you're looking up, while on the Routeburn, you're always looking down and out. On the Routeburn, you're continuously going up and down, from vast forests of beech to above tree line and then back down again. There are panoramic views of immense mountains and long valleys, million-dollar vistas everywhere you look. Though the Milford is better known, many people also place the Routeburn in the world's top ten walks."

The Routeburn Track winds through wild, mountainous country at the base of the Southern Alps, northwest of the tourist mecca of Queenstown. The track connects two of the South Island's celebrated national parks—Fiordland and Mount Aspiring—through a high pass called Harris Saddle. The main twenty-three-mile trail was officially inaugurated as a tramping destination in 1968, when the construction of four huts along the route was completed, though its human history goes back almost five hundred years further. Local Maori are believed to have traveled along the Routeburn River, moving between the Dart and Arahura Rivers, which were rich sources of pounamu—New Zealand jade. (The jade was used to make woodworking tools, weapons, and neck pendants called *hei-tiki* that are still popular in New Zealand. The World Heritage Area that encompasses much of the southern region of the South Island is known as Te Wahipounamu or "the place of greenstone.") By the 1880s, the tourism value of the Routeburn region for outdoors people had been recognized. With the establishment of

DESTINATION

30

the New Zealand Department of Tourism in the early 1900s, work began in earnest to create the trail that people know today.

Like the other eight trails that have been designated "Great Walks" by New Zealand's Department of Conservation, walks along the Routeburn Track unfold on a regulated schedule. Most trampers begin at the southern end of the track, at a spot called the Divide, and hike for three days, with two nights spent at huts en route. The Department of Conservation maintains four basic huts outfitted with gas cookers, tables, benches, cold running water, lighting, and heating in the main kitchen and dining hut, as well as bunk-rooms with mattresses. Trampers need to pack in their food. The one private concession-aire permitted to operate along the Routeburn, Ultimate Hikes New Zealand, offers more opulent digs at their two lodges along the trail at Lake Mackenzie and Routeburn Falls, including hot showers, three-course dinners and cooked breakfasts—not to mention guides well-versed in the natural and human history of the region. Wherever you rest your head, the scenic attractions of the Routeburn are the same—an astounding array of alpine peaks, pristine lakes, rich beech forests, sparkling rivers, and flora ranging from fuchsia to orchids. Those familiar with the coastal forests of the Pacific Northwest may find some similarities in the moist environs of Te Wahipounamu. But, as adventure journalist Peter Potterfield points out in *Classic Hikes of the World*, "Things down here look slightly famil-iar, but on closer inspection, unmistakably are not, so the overall effect is to give the land-scape a cockeyed look, as if one landed on a planet a lot like Earth, only different."

An early highlight comes as you make the ascent from the Divide to Key Summit (a small detour off the main track); from here, you can look down three different valleys that drain water to three different oceans, effectively a three-way continental divide. A little later on day one, a surprise awaits as you climb through a silver-beech forest. "You hear a slight rumble," Jemma described, "which increases in volume until you leave the forest and find yourself at the base of Earland Falls, which cascades more than 250 feet. As you descend toward crystal-clear Lake Mackenzie, the Hollyford Valley and snow-capped Darren Mountains unfold before you." The beeches at this lower elevation are festooned with ferns, mosses, and perching plants, and are augmented with prehistoric dragon-leaf shrubs, lending the setting an elfin aura. Six-thousand-foot Mount Emily looms above the lake.

On day two, the Routeburn climbs above tree line as you make your way up the Hollyford Face, and the forests give way to grasslands dotted with daisies, buttercups,

OPPOSITE:
The Routeburn Track offers this stunning view across Hollyford Valley to the Darren Mountains in the distance.

DESTINATION

30

Mount Cook lilies, and edelweiss. Along this section, you reach Ocean Peak Corner—from here, you can gaze the length of the Hollyford Valley, all the way to Martins Bay North on the Tasman Sea. Crossing Harris Saddle, you'll make your way down toward the upper basins of the Routeburn Valley and Mount Aspiring National Park; before your descent, you'll want to detour to Conical Hill (if the weather is conducive to long views), the highest point on the track at 5,000 feet, with correspondingly dizzying views of the Darrens. Your resting spot this evening is at Routeburn Falls. "The lodges here are right by the waterfall, and have superb views out over the valley," Jemma added. At Routeburn Falls, you're likely to encounter resident kea, an alpine parrot endemic to this region of the South Island, and renowned for their curiosity . . . and proclivity for snatching unattended food or clothing.

Your final day on the Routeburn brings you gradually down to the track's conclusion not far from the Dart River, first through the alpine pastures of Routeburn Flats and then into the gorge carved by the Routeburn River, which surges below the trail. The river's deep-green pools recall the jade that first drew the Maori here centuries before. The river temporarily disappears under a configuration of rocks known as the Sump. You'll cross it one more time on a suspension bridge at the track's end. "I had walked up to the Routeburn Falls Lodge to visit my parents, who were doing the walk from the Divide," Jemma said. "Coming back down on my own, I remember standing on that bridge, watching the river tumbling past, thinking that this was one of those 'Wow, I love my life' moments."

JEMMA KNOWLES is responsible for the sales and marketing for Ultimate Hikes. Born and raised in the UK with an adventurous spirit and a passion for the outdoors, travel, and exploration, Jemma immigrated to her favorite country, New Zealand, five years ago. Keen to let everyone know what they can experience in this truly unique environment, Jemma is proud to promote the South Island's fabulous walking adventures.

▶ **Getting There:** Queenstown, New Zealand, is generally the staging area for tramping the Routeburn Track. Air New Zealand (800-262-1234; www.airnewzealand.com) offers service to Queenstown through Air New Zealand Link via Auckland or Christchurch. There's bus service to the trailheads from Queenstown.

▶ **Best Time to Visit:** The austral spring and summer—mid-November to mid-March— provide the most reliable weather, though the season can extend a month in each direction. The New Zealand Department of Conservation regulates the number of walkers on the Routeburn Track and the hike is popular in the high season, so it's important to book ahead of time through the Great Walks Booking Office (+64 3 249-8514; www.doc.govt.nz).

▶ **Accommodations:** Destination Queenstown (+64-3-441-0700; www.queenstown-nz .co.nz) lists accommodations in the region's hub town.

▶ **Guides/Outfitters:** Ultimate Hikes New Zealand (+64-3-450-1940; www.ultimate hikes.co.nz) leads guided walks on the Routeburn, billeting clients at private (and more opulent) lodging.

DESTINATION

30

CAPE BRETON HIGHLANDS

RECOMMENDED BY **Tom Wilson**

Some hiking venues are known for their grueling week- or even month-long treks. Others boast a panoply of dawn-to-dusk, fifteen-mile, calf-busting day hikes. Cape Breton may be remembered for its rich assemblage of half-day walks. "In the Cape Breton Highlands, you can take a pleasant hike in the morning, have lunch in a Celtic pub, and do another modest hike in the afternoon," said Tom Wilson. "There are enough fine walks to keep you engaged for a weeklong holiday or more."

Cape Breton comprises the northeastern section of the Canadian province of Nova Scotia, one of the Maritimes. Bordered by the Atlantic Ocean to the east and the Gulf of St. Lawrence on the west, it's blessed with pine-covered mountains, deep river canyons, and steep cliffs that fall away to the sea; it's regularly recognized as one of the Northern Hemisphere's most beautiful islands. The Highlands encompass the northern section of the island, much of which is given over to 367-square-mile Cape Breton Highlands National Park. Thanks to a cool maritime climate and mountainous terrain, the park hosts a unique blend of Acadian, boreal, and taiga habitats. "To me, the beauty of the Highlands comes in the manner in which the mountains seem to touch the sea," Tom continued. "Many of the trails accentuate this feature."

Most of the hiking trails in the Cape Breton Highlands are situated in the national park or off the Cabot Trail, a 180-mile road that runs along the perimeter of the park and provides the less ambulatory visitor a chance to appreciate Cape Breton's many natural appeals. (The Cabot Trail, along with Glacier National Park's Going-to-the-Sun Road, is perennially ranked among the world's most spectacular road trips.) Tom shared a few of his favorite walks in the park, beginning on the east side. "Franey Trail is one that always comes to mind. It's a saucy little trail, climbing 1,400 feet in just two miles. It really gets your heart

OPPOSITE:
Sweeping coastal
vistas of the Gulf
of Saint Lawrence
and the Atlantic
Ocean await day
hikers around
Cape Breton.

DESTINATION

31

beating. When you reach the top, there are splendid views of the town of Ingonish, the Clyburn Valley, and Franey Mountain behind, and the open Atlantic before you, with Middle Head Peninsula jutting out right below into the sea. It's a two- to three-hour walk. Middle Head Trail, which starts near the historic Keltic Lodge, also has great ocean views and vistas of Cape Ingonish Island. Many people like to visit the lodge [which was commissioned by the Canadian National Park Service along with its famed adjoining golf course, Highlands Links, to attract visitors in the waning years of the Great Depression], have lunch, and then walk Middle Head, which takes less than two hours. Clyburn Valley Trail gives you a little taste of the region's history, leading out to an abandoned gold mine. The trail follows the Clyburn River and gives a glimpse of the golf course and passes some great moose habitat. In the fall, you may have a chance to glimpse Atlantic salmon in some of the Clyburn's deeper pools." (The salmon return to their natal streams to spawn; some die, some return to the sea. Their offspring, or parr, remain in the freshwater for several years before heading to sea, where they spend their adult lives before repeating the cycle of regeneration.)

If there's one walk that stands out on the west side of Cape Breton Highlands National Park, it would be the Skyline trail. A mostly level, modest four and one third miles, Skyline moves through boreal forest, ending at an overlook some 1,350 feet above the Gulf of St. Lawrence. "Words don't do justice to the views from the end of Skyline," Tom continued. "It frequently makes the cover of the Nova Scotia Tourism guide, and it's no surprise. You may see whales down below, and you're almost guaranteed to see moose. They're incredibly tame along this trail; you can walk right by them and they don't pay any attention, whereas on other trails they might charge if you were that close. For a really good workout, I'd recommend L'Acadien Trail. There's a 1,200-foot elevation gain over three miles, starting from the banks of the Chéticamp River. At the top, you can look out over the Acadian coastline as well as the Chéticamp River Valley. Black bears are often seen along this trail." If you didn't find any salmon along the Clyburn River, consider a walk on the Salmon Pools Trail along the Chéticamp, where four named pools (First, Chance, Second, and Third) often harbor fish.

Part of the allure of a hiking vacation to Nova Scotia is the chance to partake of Cape Breton's thriving Celtic culture. Though initially settled by the French in the early 1700s and then ceded to England in 1763, the flavor of Cape Breton island has been shaped most profoundly by Scottish immigrants, who arrived in the early 1800s. These Scots, forcibly displaced from the Scottish Highlands, have managed to maintain much of their way of life. While the number of citizens speaking Gaelic is shrinking, the region's culture is being passionately preserved in its music, especially a style of violin playing that's been branded "Cape Breton Fiddling".

For many hikers, the call of the trail is the chance to find solitude for contemplation, or simply silence. For others, though, hiking presents an opportunity to commune with kindred spirits who share a love of the outdoors. Walkers in the latter category will want to consider visiting Cape Breton in September during the Hike the Highlands Festival. This ten-day extravaganza features daily guided hikes, equipment and photography workshops, nightly Celtic music—and, most important, the camaraderie of like-minded folk who've traveled from across North America and Europe to attend. "I recall a hike a few years ago at the Hike the Highlands Festival," Tom added. "A group of people did the Franey Trail, and there was a lady from Scotland in the group, though I didn't realize this at the time. When we got back down to the parking lot, I heard beautiful Scottish fiddle music. I thought someone had switched on a radio, but it was the lady playing her fiddle.

"For me, this is what hiking in Cape Breton is all about: Experiencing nature and listening to music with your friends. It was the perfect ending to a hike."

TOM WILSON is the director of recreation and tourism for the Municipality of Victoria County, Cape Breton Island. An avid hiker, kayaker, cyclist, mountain biker, and amateur photographer, Tom acts as chairman for the Hike the Highlands Festival.

DESTINATION

31

If You Go

▶ **Getting There:** Air Canada (888-247-2262; www.aircanada.com) offers daily flights to Halifax, Nova Scotia, with connecting flights to Sydney, which is on the island.

▶ **Best Time to Visit:** The trails are generally clear of snow from mid-May through mid-October. Information about Cape Breton Highlands' trails and other attractions is available on the Parks Canada Web site (www.pc.gc.ca/eng/pn-np/ns/cbreton/index.aspx).

▶ **Accommodations:** The Keltic Lodge (800-565-0444; www.kelticlodge.ca) in Ingonish is the higher-end choice on the east side of the park. The Victoria County Department of Tourism website (www.visitvictoriacounty.com) lists other options.

THE AL HAJAR

RECOMMENDED BY **Tim Greening**

"In today's political climate, Yemen and Saudi Arabia are a bit wild for Westerners hoping to get a taste of Arabian culture to visit," Tim Greening began. "But Oman, on the southeastern edge of the Arabian Peninsula, is extremely friendly. You feel very comfortable there. Oman also just happens to have some brilliant treks, with very dramatic scenery. And there's no one trekking there. In five days on the trails, we saw only the odd shepherd."

The focal point of the trek is the Al Hajar Range, which runs the length of Oman's northern coastline and rise to heights of almost 10,000 feet above the sparkling waters of the Gulf of Oman. The trails through these mountains were not open to visitors until fifteen years ago, and thus have been viewed by few outsiders. The Al Hajar are at times austere and imposing, a landscape of jagged ridgelines intervening canyons parched by the region's hot, arid climate. It's in the hidden valleys, or "wadis," that much of the life of the Al Hajar transpires. Many, watered by springs or shielded from the sun by rock escarpments, appear as oases; hidden away as they are, they may seem miragelike to trekkers.

An Oman expedition begins in the capital city of Muscat—which, according to Tim, is about as far away in ambiance from the rest of Oman as you can get. "It's a sprawling, linear city, not unlike Los Angeles. There are McDonald's, Western hotels; at first you feel like you could be anywhere else in the world. But there's the Grand Mosque, which holds the largest carpet in the world; the Sultan's Palace; and the Muttrah Souk in the old port, where frankincense is burning and all the vendors are offering you tea. Suddenly, you're in Arabia." After a day of touring, visitors head south out of town in a four-wheel-drive vehicle, toward the mountains. On the outskirts of Muscat, the landscape gives way very quickly to desert. After leaving the paved roads behind, the tour climbs up and then down to the village of Wadi Bani Awf. "You drive up the main canyon, and there's a little hidden canyon down below—that's where the village is," Tim continued. "It's very much 'Indiana Jones' country, not unlike Petra in Jordan. The canyon narrows down to twenty feet, then opens up into a verdant valley, with date farms. After this first taste of wadi life, it's back in the truck, heading to the first night's camp on the Sharaf al Alamayn Plateau, and the first glimpse of the Western Hajar." Though days can be warm, reaching highs of 90 degrees, nights are generally quite cool. Tents (and other supplies) are brought from campsite to campsite by truck, leaving trekkers unencumbered.

On the third day, the caravan moves toward Jebel Shams, the highest point in Oman at 9,833 feet. "Here, we take one of Oman's most famous treks, the Balcony Route," Tim said. "The path is twenty feet wide. Below, there are massive drop-offs; above, massive cliffs. Eventually we reach a little abandoned village clinging to the rocks. The village is completely hidden from above and below. In addition to its seclusion, one can understand the appeal of such a spot—it's significantly cooler than its surroundings. Then comes the mountain of Jabul Akbar and the Wadi Al Qashah circuit, which I rank as one of the best two-day treks I've ever done. The first day is probably the hardest day of the trek. The first few hours, the ascent is quite steep, and there's a bit of scrambling involved, but eventually you get up to the rim of a fantastic gorge, and the vistas are worth it. Hiking along, you keep coming upon deserted villages—encampments from Oman's guerilla wars of the 1950s. All of them are hidden away; without a local guide, I don't think you'd come upon any of them. For that matter, it would be difficult to even follow the trail without a guide!

"For me, the evenings in the Al Hajar are very special. Omani meals often consist of small helpings of many different foods—pitas, olives, hummus, salads, mild curries of chicken or vegetables, rice. The curries are a remnant of the Indian influence on Oman from the old trading days. What really stands out for me are the stars. There's no light pollution at all here, and the sky shines brilliantly."

Following the trek down from Al Hajar, it's a day of relative indolence in Nizwa, the former capital of Oman. If Muscat seems to be heading toward a strip-mall future, Nizwa is grounded in old Arabia. "It's the kind of place where the merchants in the souks don't even take their goods in at night," Tim added. "The people of Nizwa are that honest and trusting." The craftspeople of Nizwa are especially known for their ornately engraved *khanjar*s, the short, curved daggers worn by Omani men on ceremonial occasions.

The second long trek of the trip takes place in the Eastern Hajar, and leads guests along an ancient trading route on the Selma Plateau, ending near the Gulf of Oman. "On the first day, we are mostly on top of the plateau," Tim continued. "It's not difficult hiking, but it's a long day—nine or ten hours of walking. Still, the views of the wadi below and the Ash Sharqiyah Mountains are inspirational. We camp on the plateau, and have another wonderful night of stargazing. On my last visit, there was dead wood where we camped, and we built a fire to stay warm. No one wanted to go to bed, as there was shooting star after shooting star. The second day, we drop down through the maze of Wadi Tiwi, riddled with canyons—it's a puzzle to make your way down. At the bottom, we are rewarded with big pools of clear, pure water at the village of Sooee. It's not too cold, and feels wonderful after eight hours of hiking.

"From the pools, it's a short walk to the truck, which takes us to White Beach, with its talcum-powder-soft sand. The mountains obscure the sunset, but the next morning the sun rises right out of the sea, a wonderful exclamation point on the trip."

TIM GREENING is cofounder and director of KE Adventure Travel. He has traveled to more than eighty countries around the world over the last twenty-five years, leading and researching new wilderness trips.

If You Go

▶ **Getting There:** Visitors fly into Oman's capital city, Muscat, which is served by many airlines, including KLM Royal Dutch (800-225-2525; www.klm.com) and Lufthansa (800-399-5838; www.lufthansa.com).

▶ **Best Time to Visit:** Trips are offered in November, December, and March—when Oman can be counted on to be cooler and still dry.

▶ **Guides/Outfitters:** The Al Hajar trek described above is offered by KE Adventure Travel (+44 (0) 17687 73966; www.keadventure.com).

DESTINATION

32

MOUNT HOOD NATIONAL FOREST

RECOMMENDED BY **Bill and Don Pattison**

Mountains sometimes have a way of entering one's DNA, a way of becoming part of a person, like blood and bone. On rare occasions, that mountain can become part of a whole family. This is the case for Bill and Don Pattison and their special pinnacle—Mount Hood.

"I grew up in Hood River [just north of Mount Hood, on the Columbia River], and from an early age went up to the Cooper's Spur area on the mountain to sled and toboggan with my mom and dad," Bill began. "I later learned to ski. When the GIs came back from World War II, there were a number who had been in the Tenth Mountaineering Division. They passed along their mountaineering skills to high schoolers, including me."

"And my dad, in turn, passed them on to me!" Bill's eldest son, Don, enthused. "When I was eight, my dad took my younger brother and me on a forty-odd-mile hike around Mount Hood. It's always stayed with me. I ended up working a number of years for a mountain-apparel company and volunteering with Crag Rats, an organization that conducts search-and-rescue operations on Mount Hood and the Columbia River Gorge." (Crag Rats happens to be the oldest mountain search-and-rescue organization in the United States.)

There are few more powerful symbols of the Pacific Northwest than Mount Hood, which rises majestically above the surrounding Cascade Range roughly fifty miles east of the city of Portland. At 11,239 feet, Mount Hood is the highest point in Oregon, and the fourth-highest peak in the Cascades. Like other dramatic peaks nearby, Mount Hood is a dormant volcano. Believed to have formed eleven to fourteen million years ago, Mount Hood has had at least four major eruptive periods during the past 15,000 years. One of its eruptions occurred shortly before the arrival of Lewis and Clark; the Corps of Discovery

mistook the ash from the explosion, which cluttered a local river, for quicksand, and named it accordingly—the Sandy River. Mount Hood is home to twelve glaciers, and is the source of five significant rivers, all of which eventually drain into the Columbia. From many points in north and central Oregon, Mount Hood hovers dreamlike in the distance, a postcard of alpine symmetry. (Portland residents are quite protective of their vistas of Mount Hood: After a thirty-story downtown office building was constructed in 1984, the city strengthened building regulations to protect "view corridors" so residents could look east to "their mountain.")

There are more than one hundred hiking trails on and around the mountain in the million acres of Mount Hood National Forest. For an extended walk, a favorite route is Trail 600, better known as the Timberline Trail—the forty-one-mile walk that Don first hiked as an eight-year-old. Following the tree line a full 360 degrees around the mountain, the Timberline Trail showcases alpine meadows and inspired views of the summit as hikers ford glacial streams, pass stands of ancient mountain hemlock and fir, and skirt cascading waterfalls. The vista of Coe Glacier on the north face of the mountain is especially inspiring. Another highlight of the walk is Ramona Falls, which plummets one hundred feet, shimmering against its dark basalt face with an almost phosphorescent glow. (A popular day hike takes you into Ramona Falls over the course of a seven-mile round trip.) The Timberline Trail gained some notoriety in 2004, when two of Oregon's U.S. Congressmen—Reps. Earl Blumenauer (D) and Greg Walden (R)—hiked the trail for four days (with a retinue of advisors) to gain a better understanding of the public-land-use issues facing Mount Hood. The congressmen must have come away with a deeper appreciation for the mountain the Multnomah Indians called Wy'East, as their bipartisan support helped pass the Omnibus Public Land Management Act of 2009, which gives another 127,000 acres on Mount Hood wilderness status (189,000 acres of the surrounding national forest had already been given wilderness status).

Mount Hood is said to be the second-most-climbed mountain in the world, behind only Japan's Mount Fuji. Some 10,000 climbers make the attempt each year, and Don elaborated on a few of the reasons. "Mount Hood can be done fairly easily in just a day, whereas a mountain like Rainier (also popular with unseasoned climbers) takes a three- to four-day commitment. Additionally, Hood is a fairly short climb, just three miles from the south face, and the ultimate altitude is less extreme." Bill put it more succinctly: "On a sunny day, looking up from Timberline Lodge at the peak against the cerulean sky, you

OPPOSITE: At an elevation of 11,239 feet, Mount Hood is one of the most climbed mountains in the world, and a powerful symbol of the Pacific Northwest.

DESTINATION

33

think 'I guess I'll put my sneakers on and head up.' Of course, it's a bit more complicated than that." "Mount Hood is only a stone's throw from the Pacific," Don chimed in, "and weather can move in very quickly. Having a good idea of the weather conditions is essential for your safety. Climbers who aren't well informed of the weather and get caught in a storm are the climbers who get into trouble."

There are number of ways to reach the summit of Mount Hood. The South Side route, which departs from Timberline Lodge, is the most popular for less seasoned climbers. (A story—unvalidated—goes that a woman once reached the summit on this route wearing heels!) Don and Bill prefer the Cooper Spur route, which is on the northeast side of the mountain. "You can begin from Cloud Cap Inn (a historic structure that was once operated as a hotel and now serves as headquarters for the Crag Rats)," Don continued. "You try to be moving very early—by 4 A.M.—so you're up and down before the snow softens up. The route is very direct to the summit; however, the final 2,000 feet are dangerously exposed and tiring. You follow a climbers' trail up to the top of Cooper Spur and past a prominent boulder on the ridge called Tie-in Rock. From here, you climb a forty-five-degree snow slope through 'the chimney' rock bands to the summit."

Whether you summit Mount Hood, circumnavigate the mountain, or merely complete a day hike, you'll want to pay a visit to Timberline Lodge, one of the gems of the Works Progress Administration (WPA) and Civilian Conservation Corps. The stone-and-wood edifice was built in the 1930s, almost entirely by hand, by legions of laborers and craftspeople; film buffs may recognize Timberline's exterior from *The Shining*, which doubled as the Overlook Hotel for outside shots. Today, Timberline stands as one of Oregon's most-visited tourist attractions, offering lodgings, food, and year-round skiing, plus views to the south that extend nearly a hundred miles on a clear day.

DESTINATION

33

BILL PATTISON is eighty years old and is still hiking and skiing on Mount Hood. A fourth-generation Oregonian (along with his wife, Pat), Bill has been a Hood River city councilman, mayor, and fire chief, and he owned an independent insurance agency until retirement. Bill learned to mountain climb with, and continues to be an active member of, the Crag Rats mountain-rescue organization. He has been instrumental in the restoration of the Cloud Cap Inn and the old Columbia Gorge highway. With no sign of slowing down, he's wondering when retirement actually starts.

DON PATTISON was raised in the Hood River Valley, with no choice but to accompany his family on childhood camping and ski trips. Don continues to pursue these activities to this day. He escaped the valley to attend college at Willamette University, in Salem, Oregon, and travel the world to mountain climb in his twenties. He has climbed and skied Mount McKinley and many peaks in the Alps, Himalaya, and Andes. Don now resides in Portland, Oregon, with his family, and works in the outdoor-clothing industry. He is the current president of the Hood River Crag Rats.

If You Go

▶ **Getting There:** Mount Hood is fifty miles from Portland International Airport, which is served by most major carriers.

▶ **Best Time to Visit:** Climbing season is generally May to July, though Mount Hood can be climbed at other times of the year if conditions permit. The Timberline Trail is generally free of snow from early June until late October. (Note: As of this writing, a section of the Timberline Trail is closed due to a bridge washout. There are plans to construct a new bridge.)

▶ **Accommodations:** There are a number of campgrounds in Mount Hood National Forest (www.fs.fed.us/r6/mthood). The Clackamas County Department of Tourism (800-424-3002; www.mthoodterritory.com) lists options for lodging on the mountains; some opt to stay north of Mount Hood in Hood River (www.hoodriver.org).

▶ **Guides/Outfitters:** Several outfitters lead climbs of Mount Hood, including Go Trek (503-698-1118; www.gotrek.com) and Timberline Mountain Guides (541-312-9242; www.timberlinemtguides.com).

DESTINATION

33

SNOW LAKE

RECOMMENDED BY **Dan Short**

Forget, for a moment, about the turmoil of Pakistani politics, of the machinations of corrupt generals, shadow factions, and wily tribal leaders. Look north, instead, to the wild Karakoram Mountains, home of the world's highest (and perhaps most dangerous) paved road, sixty peaks of more than 7,000 meters (22,966 feet), and the vast glacial basin that's known as Snow Lake.

OPPOSITE:
As its name implies, a good deal of the trek across Snow Lake unfolds over ice fields and hidden crevasses; it's not for the faint of heart.

"I would certainly put the trek to Snow Lake on the far end of the scale of adventure travel options," Dan Short opined. "It's for someone who's seeking an expedition-style adventure as in the days of old. Before embarking, you need to understand that the weather is not always blue-bird, and you won't always have easy days. It will test your character. But what it takes out of you never outweighs what it gives back."

The Karakoram might be thought of as "the other Himalaya," as it rests north and west of the main Himalayan Range. More than 300 miles in length, the Karakoram marks a rugged border between Pakistan, the Xinjiang province of western China, and the Ladakh region of northern India. It is one of the most glaciated regions of the world outside the Arctic, and much of the trek follows the interconnected Biafo and Hispar glaciers—a distance of some seventy-five miles—which provide a highway of sorts through the heart of the Karakoram. "It's a very committed trek," Dan continued. "Once you leave Askole (where the trek begins), there are no habitations for at least ten days. Much of the walk is at altitudes above 13,000 feet, with one camp at nearly 17,000 feet. We're often walking on glaciers, and on some of the middle portions of the trek, we must don crampons and rope up, as we're crossing crevasses, some concealed. Though it may sound daunting for the less adventurous, the trekking itself is unbelievable. This is the spiky realm of the Himalaya, and the skyline is dominated by crenellated, toppling spires

DESTINATION

34

of granite. Staring upon it at times, it's hard to fathom how it hasn't fallen down. In the Karakoram, you're in the rain shadow of the Himalaya. It's not as much of a winter scene as you find farther east."

Trekkers generally fly into Islamabad, Pakistan, and then either fly or drive to Skardu, the staging area of the trek. "Some people are hesitant about traveling to Pakistan," Dan offered, "but I believe that you're in as much danger of terrorism in London as you are in Rawalpindi. That being said, Pakistan is away from many Westerners' comfort zone." A drive on the Karakoram Highway will confirm that you're not in St. Louis or Surrey anymore. "It's a harrowing twenty-four hours," Dan continued, "but you certainly see a good deal of the country this way. I won't soon forget coming upon pick-up games of soccer or cricket on the dustbowl streets of dusky towns, or tea shops along the route. As you drink the tea, you know it might come back at you later, but you want to do it anyway, as it's such a rich cultural interaction."

Departing Askole on the trail that's used to approach K2 and Concordia mountains, your retinue cuts an impressive sight. "Trekkers in the Karakoram don't use many donkeys or yaks to haul equipment," Dan explained. "It's predominantly humans carrying your kit. We usually travel with about ten trekkers, and each trekker has three or four porters, so there's a huge train of humans going to the ice fields. The local fellows really interact with the visitors—each night, there's always a party around the fire. I recall my first crossing of Snow Lake. I was at the head of the group, falling into crevasses and marking them off. When we reached the camp at Hispar La, every one of the porters came up and shook my hand to show their gratitude for my helping to get everyone to camp safely."

The trek across Snow Lake and Hispar La is an extensive undertaking, with twenty days on the ground in Pakistan and thirteen days on the trail. The early stages of the trek, as you negotiate moraine rubble, are very strenuous. Once the Biafo Glacier is reached, the footing improves—you're walking on bare ice, but it's crenellated enough to give hikers a good grip without crampons. As mentioned above, the walk across Snow Lake requires crampons and care to avoid crevasses. The four-day descent of the Hispar Glacier presents some of the trek's most difficult walking. There's one day of roped travel on steep snow slopes, and a number of tributary glaciers must be crossed. Most of this segment of the trek, however, is off-glacier in green ablation valleys (spots where the glacier has receded). Sometimes you'll be treated to stunning wildflower displays here.

Most who've completed the Snow Lake trek agree that the highlight of the adventure is the camp on Hispar La. "We reach Hispar La after crossing Snow Lake," Dan said. "It's rare that you end up camping on such a pass, as it's high (16,895 feet) and can be quite windy. But it's such a perfect place that we have to do it. From Hispar La, you can peer down the expanse of Snow Lake to the Ogre (or Baintha Brakk, 23,895 feet), considered one of the world's most difficult mountains to scale; in the other direction are the mountains of Hunza. There's an alpine glow to Hispar La at sunrise and sunset, incredible pinks, deep cyans, and turquoises. More often than not there will be an inversion, and we'll be above the clouds.

"Before my first trip to Snow Lake, I did a great deal of reading about the area. Chris Bonnington and Doug Scott—the first mountaineers to scale the Ogre—are heroes of mine. I remember catching a glance of that mountain, and recalling their climb and even more epic descent—with broken legs, broken ribs, and a fierce week-long storm to contend with. It was an awe-inspiring feeling to walk in their footsteps."

DAN SHORT grew up inspired by the tales of explorers of earth and ocean. His first real independent experience of adventure was on the Almscliffe crag in North Yorkshire. A girlfriend once told Dan, from a crackline on that very crag, "You love rocks so much, they've replaced your brain." That relationship didn't last, but the crags inspired Dan to travel the world to see what the rest of the planet was made of. He continues to "get the juice" from the wilder places, from Kazakhstan to Libya, documenting it all with a sketchbook. Dan now calls the English Lake District, and a green VW camper called Yoda, home.

DESTINATION

(34)

If You Go

▶ **Getting There:** Islamabad, Pakistan, (your starting point) is served by many carriers, including British Airways (800-247-9297; www.britishairways.com). Your outfitter will arrange transport from Islamabad to Skardu.

▶ **Best Time to Visit:** Trips are generally led in July.

▶ **Guides/Outfitters:** KE Adventure Travel (800-497-9675; www.keadventure.com) leads several treks in the Karakoram, including to Snow Lake.

THE INCA TRAIL

RECOMMENDED BY **Alicia Zablocki**

There is debate in archeological circles regarding the role that the Lost City of the Incas— Machu Picchu—played in Inca society. Early hypotheses forwarded the notion of the citadel as a spiritual center. More recent theories have proposed that Pachucuti, the Sapa Inca (or "god emperor" of the Inca empire) had the mountain city built around 1462 as a vacation retreat of sorts. After being deserted less than one hundred years after its completion, Machu Picchu was slowly reclaimed by the jungle; its temples, residences, and interconnected water fountains were masked from the world until 1911, when they were rediscovered by an American historian, Hiram Bingham. Nearly as remarkable as Machu Picchu's polished-stone construction (with no use of mortar or other adhesive materials) and cloud-forest setting is the fact that it exists at all: Pizarro and his fellow Spaniards laid waste to a majority of Inca structures, and actively searched for Machu Picchu, believing it to contain untold riches.

"I had visited Machu Picchu when I was young, though I went by train," Alicia Zablocki recalled. "When I had the chance to hike the trail many years later, I didn't know what to expect. I was a little intimidated by the altitudes, as I hadn't done a lot of long-distance hiking before, and none at high elevations. Once you get started, though, you don't think much about it—as long as you're in decent shape and have the right attitude, you'll do fine. The ruins were everything that I remembered and perhaps even more thanks to my adult perspective, but what really has stayed with me was the hike itself. The many different microenvironments you walk through, the size of the mountains, and the trail itself, with the intricately laid stones. For me, it was surreal."

The Inca Trail is a walking route that traces a section of the path of an old Inca roadway that led from Cuzco to Machu Picchu, in the Andes of southern Peru. At the height

OPPOSITE:
The magnificent, mysterious ruins at Machu Picchu are a fitting reward for trekkers who reach the end of the Inca Trail.

DESTINATION

35

of the Inca empire, there were nearly 14,000 miles of trails crisscrossing South America, a road system stretching from Colombia to northern Argentina. Some of the paths were twenty-five feet wide, others barely a yard. The Inca Trail—at least as taken by modern-day trekkers—begins at the town of Piskacucho, and stretches some twenty-nine miles. It would be a memorable trek even if the fabled settlement did not wait at the end. The scenery is breathtaking; hiking above the rushing Urubamba and Cusichaca Rivers, you'll pass through rain forests and cloud forests, and along the edge of the Vilcanota Ridge, where Veronica Peak reaches 19,000 feet. There are smaller ruins to explore along the way as you build toward your arrival at Machu Picchu. Distances—averaging around nine miles a day—are not exceptionally long, but the trail begins at an elevation of nearly 9,000 feet, and some days you'll gain as much as 4,000 feet. As Alicia mentioned, you need not be in excellent physical condition to trek the Inca Trail, though if you're prop-erly acclimatized to the altitude (best achieved by spending a day or two at elevation before the trek begins), the pace is relaxed enough for individuals of average athleticism to keep up . . . especially since many hikers will end up retaining a porter to help with the heavy lifting. A good interpretive guide can add an extra dimension to the trip, from describing the Incan method for cultivating potatoes to explaining the historic relevance of ruins along the trail.

The trek up the Inca Trail builds in intensity as it approaches its climax. Day two serves up the most challenging trekking, as you cross Abra Warmihuañusca, "Dead Woman's Pass," at 13,776 feet; domesticated llamas and alpacas are often seen grazing here on the puna (Andean grasslands). Hummingbirds will escort you through the cloud forest as you descend to Pacaymayo Valley and camp. Day three may be the most interest-ing hike of the trip, with a number of archeological sites along the way. Near the moun-tain pass of Abra de Runkurakay, there's a small oval structure that's believed to have served as a watchtower. Coming down off the pass, you reach Sayacmarca. This complex has a semicircular construction, enclosures at different levels, narrow streets, liturgical fountains, patios, and irrigation canals. One of the best-preserved sites on the trail is Phuyupatamarca, or "town at the edge of the clouds." From above the ruins, you can take in a complex of water fountains (believed to have been used for sacred rituals) and sweep-ing views of the Urubamba River valley.

On day four, you will cover the last few miles of the trail and have the opportunity to gaze upon the citadel of Machu Picchu, the only known Inca city that remains virtually intact. Some will rise well before dawn, walking with headlamps to reach Inti Punku, the "Gate of the Sun," in time for sunrise. Others may sleep in a bit and let anticipation build. Whatever lighting conditions you find, your first glimpse of Machu Picchu will be astounding. "I reached the Gate of the Sun in the afternoon, and the sight of Machu Picchu below was simply amazing," Alicia reminisced. "Some of the people in my group had tears in their eyes as they looked down.

"My favorite vista of Machu Picchu is from the peak of Huayna Picchu, which rises above the ruins at an elevation close to 9,000 feet. It's about a three-hour hike from the ruins and steep at times, but it provides a completely different vantage point of the citadel, and really highlights the grandeur of the Andes, and how difficult building Machu Picchu must have been.

"Gazing at Machu Picchu, I'm left with more questions than answers."

ALICIA ZABLOCKI is program director for Mountain Travel Sobek. In her 25 years in the adventure travel industry she traveled the world, particularly around South America. Alicia has hiked the Inca Trail three times: the Cordillera Blanca, the Cordilla Huayhuash, and the Cordillera Vilcabamba.

If You Go

▶ **Getting There:** Cuzco, Peru, is the staging area for hiking the Inca Trail; Cuzco is served from Lima by several airlines, including LAN Airlines (866-435-9526; www.lan.com).

▶ **Best Time to Visit:** It's possible to hike the Inca Trail throughout the year (with the exception of February, when the trail is maintained). Many opt to hike during the dry season—April to October. August is the busiest month on the Trail.

▶ **Guides/Outfitters:** Peruvian officials require that hikers on the Inca Trail be accompanied by a guide. There are outfitters who lead Inca Trail adventures, including Mountain Travel Sobek (888-831-7526; www.mtsobek.com).

DESTINATION

35

VOLCANOES NATIONAL PARK

RECOMMENDED BY **Jeanie Fundora**

Rwanda has been scarred in the popular imagination by the civil wars that have wracked this small landlocked nation in Equatorial Africa. Many may not realize that this mountainous country—dubbed the "Land of a 1,000 Hills"—is home to a biped that's far less belligerent—and far more rare—than *Homo sapiens*: the mountain gorilla.

"Primate safaris are unique because they can only be done in a few places in the world," Jeanie Fundora began. "If you're hoping to observe mountain gorillas, your options are even more finite, limited to the Virunga Mountains, which run along the northern border of Rwanda and in Uganda's Bwindi Impenetrable National Park. There are no specimens held in captivity anywhere in the world. When we sought to assemble a trip that would include mountain gorillas, Volcanoes National Park in Rwanda was the obvious choice. It's not as strenuous as the Impenetrable Forest, and you're almost guaranteed to see these wonderful animals."

The civil unrest that once spilled into Volcanoes National Park (its headquarters were attacked by rebels in 1992) has been quelled, and since 1999, visitors have been able to safely return. Situated in the far northwest of Rwanda, the park protects the steep slopes of the five volcanoes of the Virunga Range that rest in the country—Sabyinyo, Muhabura, Gahinga, Bisoke, and the tallest (at 14,787 feet), Karisimbi. The forest here is a pastiche of flowering plants (*Lobelia*, *Hagenia abyssinica*, and *Neoboutonia*), evergreen, and bamboo, and is home to a number of extraordinary animals, including endangered golden monkeys, spotted hyena, and a number of different birds, including nearly thirty species and subspecies endemic to the region. But it's the mountain gorillas that rule the forest here, drawing a finite, fortunate group of visitors. Volcanoes National Park was the site where naturalist Dian Fossey conducted her research on mountain gorillas from 1967 to

OPPOSITE: The Virunga Mountains are a stronghold of the mountain gorilla.

DESTINATION

36

1985, and her promotion of their plight very likely helped save the animals from extinction. (Her book about her experiences, *Gorillas in the Mist*, was later made into a movie of the same name. Fossey was murdered in her home in 1985, likely by the poachers she bravely battled.) It's believed that approximately 320 mountain gorillas live in the Virunga range, with 340 animals in Bwindi.

Most visitors to Volcanoes National Park fly into Rwanda's capital city of Kigali, a two-and-a-half-hour ride from the park headquarters. Not far from Kigali, you'll begin to reach the thickly wooded, mountainous Africa that both frightened and titillated Europeans, the "deepest, darkest Africa" that was last to be explored. Upon reaching headquarters, you'll meet your guides for the day. "It works like this," Jeanie explained. "The National Park sends trackers out at sunrise to locate the groups of gorillas—there are five or six groups in Volcanoes National Park that are habituated to visitors. Once the groups are located, the trackers radio back to park headquarters with a location. Having the trackers not only helps insure that we'll find animals; it also helps the park service keep a day-to-day tally of the animals, so any poaching can be quickly identified. National Park officials will assign you to a group, with no more than seven or eight clients per group (there's a limit of forty visitor permits issued a day). The guides that accompany us know all the villagers, and there's interaction with the local people. One of the guides—François—worked with Dian Fossey. He's a walking encyclopedia.

"The hike in can be anywhere from half an hour to four hours, and the terrain is beautiful—very mountainous, with verdant forests with bamboo trees and wild celery. Once you reach the trackers, who stay nearby the gorilla group once they've located it, you're asked to leave behind any jackets or backpacks. The sound of zippers makes the gorillas anxious, and you don't want them getting angry. You're also told to avoid eye contact with the gorillas, as they may take this as a challenge." Female mountain gorillas can reach four feet in height with a weight of 300 pounds; males reach a maximum height of six feet and can weigh 500 pounds, and develop a patch of grayish hair on their backs at maturity, hence their "Silverback" sobriquet. They are extremely powerful.

"Once you've shed any zippered items and disengaged your flash, you can approach the gorillas with your guide," Jeanie continued. "You're usually within twenty feet. Guests are not allowed to touch the animals, though the babies will often come up and sock you on the leg. You have to stand there and take it, as the mother and males are watching. My favorite visits are those that have involved groups with younger animals. In one group, there was a little guy—about a year and a half old, our guide thought—that had hair like the singer Rod Stewart. He went around harassing each adult gorilla in the group, climbing up on the Silverbacks' heads, wreaking havoc—much like a human child. In that same group, there was a mother with a very new baby. I was straining to see the baby, and she noticed. Finally, she gave me a threatening stare and turned around to shield him from my gaze. It was very apparent that she shared the same maternal instincts as human mothers feel." Volcanoes National Park visitors are allotted two one-hour sessions over two days with the park's mountain gorillas. The park takes the time allotments seriously; guides are outfitted with stopwatches to time each one-hour visit.

JEANIE FUNDORA is the Africa product manager for Cox and Kings USA. She is an insatiable world traveler and photographer. She has traveled extensively throughout sub-Saharan Africa and the Indian Ocean Islands, and affectionately calls Africa her second home, as this is truly what it has become to her.

If You Go

▶ **Getting There:** Kigali, Rwanda, is served by several carriers, including Brussels Airlines (+32 2 723 2345; www.brusselsairlines.com).

▶ **Best Time to Visit:** Thanks to its high altitude, Rwanda has a clement climate year-round. The driest months—July to September—are preferred.

▶ **Accommodations:** The town of Musanze is just outside Volcanoes National Park, and many park visitors will stage here. The Rwanda Tourism Board's Web site (www.rwanda tourism.com) lists lodgings options.

▶ **Guides/Outfitters:** Permits are necessary to visit the mountain gorillas and are available from the Rwanda Tourism Board (+25 0 57 6514; reservation@rwandatourism.com); a very finite number of permits are available each day. Many tour operators can help you coordinate a gorilla trek. Cox and Kings (800-999-1758; www.coxandkingsusa.com) orchestrates gorilla treks as part of their Great Ape Safari.

MOUNT TRIGLAV

RECOMMENDED BY **Kit Wilkinson**

For Slovenians, Triglav is much more than a mountain: it's a central component of the national identity. The three summits of Triglav rise in tremendous relief from the surrounding foothills, nearly 6,000 feet above the adjoining valleys. (There's some dispute about the origin of its name—some believe it speaks to the mountain's three heads, others think it's a paean to a complex of gods from Slavic mythology.)

During Slovenia's annexation under the republic of Yugoslavia, the mountain was a symbol of rebellion as Slovenians struggled for liberation. Once Yugoslavia dissolved and Slovenia became an independent nation, it emblemized the country's newfound sovereignty. A silhouette of Triglav is the centerpiece of the Slovenian flag, and decorates the fifty-eurocent coin. Picking up on this symbol of national solidarity, the first president of Slovenia, Milan Kučan, pronounced that it is the obligation of every Slovenian to climb Mount Triglav at least once. "This may explain why there were people of all shapes and sizes puffing up Triglav the last time I was there," Kit Wilkinson said. "Some were being hauled by their better halves. Many of the Slovenians were not your typical alpinists."

Slovenia is a republic whose identity—let alone location—may be little known to North Americans. The small mountainous nation is on the Balkan Peninsula, bordered by Austria to the north, Hungary to the northeast, Croatia to the south and southeast, and Italy and the Adriatic Sea to the west. Situated between Eastern and Western Europe, Slovenia strikes a happy balance between the Italian, Austrian, and Slavic cultures that have come to bear upon it. (The conflicts and ethnic unrest that have plagued the other republics that once formed Yugoslavia have been absent here.) "Slovenia has a very similar feel to mountain Italy or Austria," Kit continued. "This is true of the scenery, and also of the little guest houses and taverns. It is, after all, a continuation of the Alps."

164

The limestone peaks of the Julian Alps are an extension of the central European Alps, and dominate the northwestern portion of Slovenia. Though not quite as high as the Alps to the west (Mount Triglav, the highest peak, has an elevation of 9,397 feet), the rugged Julians are tailor-made for walking, serving up a smorgasbord of alpine pasture, pine forest, clear streams—and long ridgelines offering expansive vistas. Much of the Julians are contained in Triglav National Park, Slovenia's only national park. At 340 square miles, the park comprises 3 percent of the young nation's total landmass, and is home to chamois, ibex, red deer, and, occasionally, brown bear and lynx. Triglav is also home to some fifty-two mountain huts, making it ideal for a trekking holiday. "The huts in Triglav are quite nice," Kit commented. "They're not quite hotels, but they're close. They're situated in sensational spots, perched in the middle of the karst cliffs. Some have private rooms, all have a restaurant and a bar with an outside terrace that serves beer and wine." The lodges are very reasonably priced, and serve hearty Slovenian meals like *enolončnica* (a vegetable-and-pork stew) and *jesprenj* (barley gruel).

It's possible to make an assault on Mount Triglav in just a few days, should you be under time constraints, though if you've made it this far, Kit encourages a more leisurely approach. "You start from the lakeside town of Bled, one of alpine Europe's most picturesque towns. On the first day of walking, you follow the Sava Bohinjka River, gradually gaining elevation as you pass through woodland and alpine meadows. The next few days, the trail follows a series of high ridge lines, above lush valleys. The contrast between the stark karst hillsides and green valleys is very pleasing. On the fourth day, the trail drops into the Valley of the Seven Lakes. Each of the lakes has a different shade of water, and modest elevation changes make this a more restful day as you build toward summit day. The next day brings you into Trenta Valley, where you'll be treated to a startling view of Triglav looming above. This night, you'll stay at the Kredarica Hut, just 800 feet below the summit. Anticipation is high as the sun sets on the great mountain."

To make your ascent of Triglav, you will have help in the form of the *via ferrata*. The *via ferrata* ("iron road" in Italian) provides a series of rungs, rails, and cables that permit hikers lacking technical rock-climbing experience to scale rock faces that would otherwise be beyond their skill. While their origin is often credited to the Italian army (which attached permanent lines and ladders in the Dolomites during World War I to move troops and equipment), evidence suggests that the first *via ferrata* were developed in Austria nearly eighty years earlier. The Italian Alpine Club certainly popularized their recreational use, and expanded the number of *via ferrata* routes; today, there are more than 300 around the world. "To use the *via ferrata* on Mount Triglav, you wear a harness that has two ropes equipped with carabiners," Kit explained. "If you slip and fall a foot or two, the carabiners hold. If you take a bigger fall, they have an expansion facility, and the ropes absorb the impact. The *via ferrata* make getting to the top of Triglav fairly easy. You never get beyond scrambling."

As you make your way up the final narrow ridge to the highest of Mount Triglav's three peaks, buoyed by *via ferrata*, the surrounding valleys and serrated peaks of the Julian Alps come into sharp focus. Before you descend, be sure to pause by Aljaž Tower, a small metal structure that honors Jakob Aljaž, a priest (and mountaineer) who purchased the mountaintop for the Slovene people more than a hundred years ago. Your photo by the tower may just gain you honorary Slovenian citizenship.

KIT WILKINSON is a keen fell-runner and photographer, and has been involved in the production of every KE Adventure Travel brochure since 1988. Some of his other favorite places include Iceland, Niger, and Nepal's wild western district of Dolpo.

If You Go

▶ **Getting There:** Visitors to Triglav National Park generally fly into the capital city of Ljubljana, Slovenia, which is served by many airlines, including Air France (800-237-2747; www.airfrance.com).

▶ **Best Time to Visit:** The most popular visiting time is July through mid-October; later-season visitors will see lighter crowds.

▶ **Accommodations:** The Bled tourism website (www.bled.si/en) outlines lodging options in this picturesque town. Contact Triglav National Park (+386 4 578 02 00; www.tnp.si) for details about mountain-hut lodging.

▶ **Guides/Outfitters:** A number of outfitters lead trips to Triglav, including KE Adventure Travel (800-497-9675; www.keadventure.com). If you go it alone, it's recommended that you hire a guide from Triglav National Park.

THE KING'S TRAIL

RECOMMENDED BY **Bob Carter**

The Kungsleden (or "King's Trail") is Scandinavia's best-known trail, running 265 miles north to south along Sweden's border with Norway. It was not created by or for Swedish royalty, but instead gained its sobriquet from its reputation among aficionados as a king among trails. (The route was created by the Swedish Tourist Association at the end of the nineteenth century to introduce both down country Swedes and foreign hikers to the majesty of Lapland.) For some Swedish nationals, it's a point of national pride to hike the entire trail, either in a monthlong odyssey or in a series of one-week walks. Visitors generally trek the northernmost fifty-four miles, which run from Abisko to Kebnekaise Mountain Station, above the Arctic Circle, through a sublime landscape of birch forests, jagged mountain peaks, immense glaciers, deep valleys, and turbulent river rapids.

"In some ways, the King's Trail gives you the best of both worlds," Bob Carter began. "It puts you in the middle of western Europe's last great wilderness, with tremendous wide-open spaces and stunning scenery. Thanks to the infrastructure of the trail and mountain huts, the wilderness is accessible to walkers with less wilderness experience. I spent a lot of time in Scotland before coming to the King's Trail, and I'd liken this part of Lapland to the Highlands, but on a much bigger scale; not bigger mountains, but just bigger. Sections of the King's Trail run past Sarek National Park, which has no trails or other infrastructure and is completely wild. You can stay at one of the cabins along the King's Trail and make detours into Sarek."

After a gentle first day along the beech-lined Abisko River, the King's Trail climbs above tree line. The Kebnekaise massif, Sweden's tallest mountain (with the Kebne peak eclipsing 6,900 feet) will be in view for much of the remaining time on the trail. (Hikers have the option of climbing to the top of Kebne near the trek's conclusion.) The terrain is rugged—

sweeping, glaciated valleys (like Tjäktjavagge), shimmering glaciers, and moonscape-like passes—but the walking is not overly taxing. "Daily distances on this section of the King's Trail range from ten to fifteen miles," Bob explained. "While you need to be accustomed to carrying a modest backpack—twenty-five to thirty pounds—you never gain more than 1,000 feet of elevation on any one day. Boggy areas have boardwalks above them to protect the terrain and keep hikers comfortable, and larger streams have suspension bridges. There's no need to feel rushed along the Kungsleden in the summer—light lingers in the sky through most of the night. You can go for a hike at one a.m. if you desire, and you'll have no problem finding your way."

The mountain huts along the King's Trail provide a perfect middle path between camping and a proper lodge. "The huts are very well designed to blend in with the landscape and not detract from the wilderness experience," Bob said. The wooden structures include sleeping rooms (with bunk beds), a common room, and a kitchen. Each room is equipped with a wood-burning stove; a well-stocked woodshed rests outside, as well as an outhouse and the living quarters of the *stugvard*, the hut's volunteer caretaker. (It's accepted courtesy on the Kungsleden to restock firewood and tidy up the hut before hitting the trail.) The huts have gas stoves for cooking, as well as running water, though that running water is in the form of streams that run a hundred yards or so away; while mildly inconvenient, the water is pure enough to drink without treatment. At the Alesjaure Mountain Hut complex, you'll find the first of several saunas along the trail. The dry warmth is a well-deserved reward.

The wilderness of northern Norrbotten county is home to an abundance of animal life, including brown bear, lynx, wolf, wolverine, and moose. "The moose in Sarek are Sweden's largest," Bob said. "The genetic strains produce gigantic bulls, though they're seldom seen." The two animals you're most likely to encounter, however, are lemmings and the iconic ungulate of the Arctic, the reindeer. In the summer, reindeer feed on grass and leaves; in the winter, they feed on lichens (mostly from fir-spruce trees) and shrubs, but mostly subsist on fat reserves. Most of the reindeer that hikers encounter on the King's Trail are semidomesticated, herded by the Sami, the indigenous people of Swedish Lapland (which they call *Sápmi*). "Sometimes we'll come upon the nomadic villages of the Sami," Bob added, "a series of *kata*, the tepee-type of structure that they use for shelter. If we do, we can stop off and visit, and perhaps buy handicrafts, which, as you might expect, are connected to reindeer. The Sami are renowned for their sense of humor. My

OPPOSITE:
The Kungsleden (or King's Trail) winds through the middle of western Europe's last great wilderness.

DESTINATION

38

wife was visiting one of their fixed camps recently, and the villagers had set up a reindeer-burger bar called 'Lapdonald's.'"

As mentioned above, more adventurous trekkers may wish to detour into Sarek National Park to experience the Swedish wilderness without the comforts of huts, board-walks, and trails. Bob recalled one such adventure. "One of the popular hikes in the Sarek is to a hill called Nammatj. From here, you have a fantastic view over the Rapa Valley delta, where many of the region's glacier-fed rivers come together. To do this hike, you take a short trip upriver in a boat that's operated by a Sami guide. I was going upriver to the hike on one occasion, and was joined in the boat by a pair of Dutch fellows with huge rucksacks. One of the guys had a T-shirt that said 'Wildebeest Trekking.' I was sitting next to the guide, and he was chuckling to himself as we motored along. I asked him 'What's funny?' in Swedish. He replied that he often brings big men with big ruck-sacks into the Sarek wilderness, but when he goes to pick them up the following week, they look much smaller."

BOB CARTER started Nature Travels with his wife, Sofia, in 2005; the company orches-trates a variety of outdoor experiences throughout Sweden. Bob has long been fascinated with the outdoor wonders Sweden has to offer, and has kayaked, dog-sledded, hiked, and skied across much of the Scandinavian nation.

If You Go

▶ **Getting There:** Kungsleden visitors tend to fly into Kiruna, Sweden, which has regular service from Stockholm on SAS (800-221-2350; www.flysas.com). From Kiruna, it's one and a half hours by car to Abisko Turiststation where the trek begins.

▶ **Best Time to Visit:** Hikes on the Kungsleden are offered from late June through mid-September. You can cross-country ski the trail in the winter months. Learn more about the trail from the Swedish Tourist Association (+44 08-463 21 00; www.svenskaturist-foreningen.se).

▶ **Guides/Outfitters:** Nature Travels (+44 1929 463774; www.naturetravels.co.uk) leads hiking trips on the Kungsleden, through Sarak National Park, and in other venues in Sweden.

THE HAUTE ROUTE

RECOMMENDED BY **Sean Morrissey**

Sean Morrissey still vividly remembers his first glimpse of the Matterhorn. "I was seventeen years old, hitchhiking my way from England toward the Alps for my first season of rock and mountain climbing. At the village of Tesch in the valley leading up to Zermatt, the roads stopped and we had to catch a train for the final few miles up into Zermatt. We didn't think we were experienced enough to climb the Matterhorn, but we hoped to at least see it.

"On the train ride, you had beautiful views out over the valleys, and we were constantly leaning out of the window, hoping to catch a glimpse of the great mountain. We had vistas of Breithorn and Monte Rosa, but the Matterhorn was never in sight. We were becoming desperate for a glance, yet even when the train arrived in Zermatt, the massif was not in view. We left the train and began walking up the main street, toward St. Peter's Church. When we reached the church, we looked up and had our first view, an amazing chocolate-box kind of view—this big horn, very dark, a plume of clouds hanging over it. I remember being scared and awed at the same time, moved by its utter verticality."

Since British mountaineer Edward Whymper first summited the Matterhorn—a spire that rises 9,000 feet directly above Zermatt—in 1865, alpinists from around the world have flocked to the town to make their ascent. Even more hikers have made the trek here simply to lay eyes upon the Matterhorn, and their preferred trail has been the Haute Route, which leads from Chamonix, France (home of Mont Blanc), to Zermatt, via ten or more high Alpine passes. (The basic trail was originally dubbed the High Level Route by Whymper's Anglo contemporaries at the Alpine Club. Its designation *en français* took hold after a group of French adventurers successfully skied the route in

1911.) The hikers' Haute Route, generally traversed in somewhere between eight days and two weeks, provides an exhilarating overview of the Alps, alternating from barren tarns and craggy passes to verdant meadows and heartbreakingly beautiful alpine hamlets. It's a rigorous trek—many days involve ten miles or more, with ascents and descents of more than 2,000 feet at elevations of more than 6,000 feet—but the rewards are more than commensurate for your efforts.

"The first week of the hike crosses stark, high mountain territory," Sean explained. "You're crossing the grain of the land, along ridgelines. Around Verbier and Montfort, it's a bit like a moonscape. There are few other hikers along this section, but there are chamois and ibex. The trails in this section are difficult to follow, and though there are several refuges, you don't want to be caught along this stretch in bad weather. (Visitors on guided hikes sleep at inns and hotels in valleys along the route.) Toward the conclusion of the first week, you reach the Pas de Chèvre, which leads down into the Swiss village of Arolla. From this pass—if the skies are clear—you get a tantalizing glimpse of the tip of the Matterhorn. It's not the classical view people anticipate, which makes it even more interesting. If I'm leading a tour, I'll announce, 'There it is—but we still have a week to go.' Arolla is a very traditional village in the Swiss canton of Valais, and we'll generally have a rest day here, kicked off by an amazing Swiss dinner—raclette (melted cheese with gherkins and potatoes), chilled Swiss white wine, and an after-dinner liqueur called *Kirsch* (a powerful clear liquor made from local cherries that aids the digestion of all that cheese). I like to stay at the Grand Hotel Kurhaas, which seems like something out of a Sherlock Holmes story. Throughout the hotel, there are old photographs of Victorian ladies clad in hoop skirts, going off mountain climbing."

The second half of the Haute Route Trail is decidedly more verdant than the first half. "I like to call it the Julie Andrews week," Sean joked. "There are intimate trails winding through green hills and amazing little Swiss villages. During this phase of the hike, you'll experience some of Switzerland's most beautiful trails. From Arolla in the Val d' Herens we make the crossing of the Col de Torrent, a steady ascent over grassy flower-filled pastures, with magnificent views over the snowcapped mountains. The top offers jaw-dropping, panoramic views of the region's many 13,000+ foot peaks, even the distant Mont Blanc, a grand panorama equal to almost anything seen so far. You descend into Grimentz, a fairytale village in the lovely Val d' Anniviers. Grimentz is one of the most striking of the villages on the Haute Route with its little wooden houses, each

OPPOSITE:
The Haute Route offers tantalizing glimpses of the Matterhorn long before you reach Zermatt.

DESTINATION

39

173

decorated with flower boxes. It's frequently recognized as one of Europe's best-kept villages."

Most of the trails of the Haute Route have been used for centuries by animal herders, religious pilgrims, and villagers. Near the route's conclusion, however, you have the option to walk a new trail from the burg of Grachen to Zermatt, the Europaweg. "It's a lovely balcony trail on the far side of the valley, quite challenging but with spectacular views across the Mattertal Valley," Sean said. "From here, you'll get your first clear view of the Matterhorn. Oddly enough, there didn't used to be any good trails from Grachen to Zermatt. Most people would get on the train for the final dozen miles or so up into Zermatt. While you can do the stretch in a long day, most people opt to spend a night at the new Europa Hut, which is halfway along the trail."

Once you reach Zermatt, there's a chance to relax and savor your achievement . . . or to embark on some stunning day hikes. Of these, the most popular is Hörnü Hut, the starting point for mountaineers questing for the summit of the Matterhorn. "Hörnü Hut is on a ridge right at the base of the mountain," Sean described. "As you hike up, the spire of the Matterhorn looms above you. If you get there at lunchtime, you can sit out on the deck in the shadow of the mountain, watching climbers who set out at two o'clock that morning making their way back down. They're just little dots of bright clothing. If you linger a bit later into the afternoon, those climbers start coming into the lodge, ready to celebrate, and the beer and wine start flowing! Technically, the Matterhorn is not that difficult to climb; if conditions are perfect, almost anyone who's a good hiker can do it. But generally the weather's not that cooperative. Most people climb in the company of a Swiss guide. It's a one-on-one climb, and the guides insist that guests climb another mountain in the area before they climb the Matterhorn to make sure of their stamina and ability."

One of Sean's favorite day hikes out of Zermatt is the trek up the Mettelhorn, a modest mountain (by this region's standards) of 11,175 feet that juts upward from the eastern side of town. "On the other side of Zermatt, you can take a tram or chairlift up to trailheads to begin your hike," Sean explained. "On the Mettelhorn side of the valley, you have to hike. Setting out from near the church, you soon leave the village and its ski lifts and bierstubes behind as you follow good trails up small side valleys and across alpine plateaus to the summit. It's an ascent of 5,000 feet, at the edge of what many would consider a day hike. But the reward is a stunning view of fifty or sixty of the highest peaks in the Alps (from a total of eighty-six) that eclipse 4,000 meters. I've started out when the weather was misty, and you couldn't see anything. Then at one point in the hike, you're suddenly above the weather, looking over the clouds at these immense peaks."

SEAN MORRISSEY was born and raised in London but also spent time in Ireland with relatives while growing up (he holds both Irish and British passports). He moved to Australia at age twenty, worked there for two years, then heeded the call of the mountains and became a professional guide. In summer, he guides and climbs in the Alps and in fall and spring he heads to the Himalaya for trekking and expeditions in Nepal, Bhutan, and Tibet. "I love camping, which is good because in my early guiding years, I spent more than 300 nights a year in a tent! The life of a guide really agrees with me. What's better than meeting new clients and people from all over the world, building on those relationships, and spending time outdoors in the world's best mountain regions?" Sean cooks a mean curry, is passionate about the environment, enjoys sharing ideas about how the world works, and, above all else, is a consummate professional who understands what it takes to run a great trip. He lives in Bend, Oregon, with his wife and fellow guide, Leila Thompson.

If You Go

▶ **Getting There:** Most Haute Trail expeditions begin at Chamonix, France, or Grig, Switzerland. Visitors generally fly into Geneva or Zurich (served by most major carriers) and reach the Simplon Pass area via train.

▶ **Best Time to Visit:** The Haute Trail is usually clear of snow by mid-June.

▶ **Guides/Outfitters:** Many travel companies lead expeditions covering varying portions of the Haute Trail, including Wilderness Travel (800-368-2794; www.wildernesstravel .com). Several companies, including Distant Journeys (888-845-5781; www.distantjourneys .com) can help you assemble a self-guided trip, including inn and hut reservations.

DESTINATION

39

MOUNT KILIMANJARO

RECOMMENDED BY **Ally Burnett**

In a final reverie toward the conclusion of "The Snows of Kilimanjaro," the short story's protagonist, Harry, imagines a trip to the great mountain:

> Compie turned his head and grinned and pointed and there, ahead, all he could see, as wide as all the world, great, high and unbelievably white in the sun, was the square top of Kilimanjaro. And then he knew that that was where he was going.

Hemingway's Harry never made it to Uhuru Peak, the highest point on Kilimanjaro at 19,336 feet. But if you're in decent physical condition and are not prone toward altitude sickness, the ceiling of Africa, in all its unlikely snowy grandeur, is within reach with just a walking stick and a pair of sturdy boots . . . and a good deal of determination.

"I had climbed other mountains before, but I felt that ascending Kilimanjaro would push my limits," Ally Burnett said. "I wanted to prove to myself that I could endure the hardships of the climb—though perhaps 'hardship' isn't exactly the right word. At the time I hiked Kilimanjaro, I was working for the luxury-travel company Abercrombie and Kent. A bunch of A&K employees did the climb for a charity event, and it was done in typical A&K style. We had eighty-seven porters for fourteen hikers. They lugged portable toilets, proper camp beds, a nicely appointed kitchen tent. We were quite a spectacle making our way up the mountain—other trekkers were taking pictures as we walked past."

No other landmark signifies East Africa like Mount Kilimanjaro, the tallest freestanding mountain in the world. The massif, on the northern border of Tanzania overlooking Kenya, rises more than 16,700 feet from the surrounding plains, and consists of three volcanoes—Kibo, Mawenzie, and Shira. (Kibo and Mawenzie still have intact rims and

OPPOSITE:
At 19,336 feet, Mount Kilimanjaro is Africa's tallest mountain, the "ceiling of the continent."

DESTINATION

40

calderas; Shira has collapsed.) Though nearly adjacent to Serengeti National Park, one should not climb Kilimanjaro expecting to encounter Africa's Big Five. Instead, one makes the climb for the satisfaction of conquering one of the Seven Summits (a sobriquet for the tallest peaks on each continent).

There are six routes to Uhuru Peak—Marangu, Machame, Rongai, Lemosho, Umbwe, and Shira. Of the six, Marangu (often called the "Coca-Cola Route") is the most popular because it is the least taxing hike, and affords climbers mountain-hut accommodations where the ubiquitous American soft drink is available; it's the default choice for non-guided hikers. Ally's group (perhaps buoyed by their army of porters!) opted for the Machame Route—sometimes called the "Whisky Route," presumably to imply that this trail requires more machismo than the soft-drink path. While perhaps not as comfortable as Marangu, most would say that Machame is the most scenic route. Summiting of Kilimanjaro via Machame can be accomplished in six days, though adding a seventh day allows for extra altitude acclimatization. "My group's biggest worry as we started out was whether anyone would suffer from altitude sickness," Ally recalled. "Fortunately, we all made it. I suffered a bit early on, but as I got higher, my body adjusted."

The climb to the summit of Kibo has been described as a "climatic world tour," taking you from equatorial Africa to the Arctic in less than a week. From cultivated farmlands at the foot of the mountain, you ascend to lush montane forest, then onto a moorland area of heather that's dotted with gigantic lobelias. Soon all but the most spartan vegetation disappears as you enter an arid moonscapelike terrain at an elevation of 13,000 feet, which then gives way to the snow and ice of the upper mountain. The toughest day before the final summit ascent is day four, the trek from Shira to Barranco. "Some call this the 'walk high, sleep low' day," Ally continued. "You get up to 15,000 feet at the Lava Tower, and then drop back down to camp at 13,000 feet. It's a long day, but it helps with your acclimatization." The next day, hikers ascend the Barranco Wall and make their way to Karanga, which offers a spectacular view of the glaciers above, which take on a deep red shade in the evening light. From Karanga, it's a half-day walk to Barafu, where it's good to rest up for the night's climb.

Ally's final push for the summit began around midnight. "We'd gone to bed very early that evening, but I don't think that any of us really slept," she recalled. "Leaving Barafu Camp (at 15,000 feet), the climb was quite difficult. The path is on shale, and very steep. I had to take very small steps and work hard to keep from sliding back. It being the middle of the night, I couldn't see the path we were treading on. All that was visible was a procession of headlamps—very memorable! We hiked for five or six hours without a break. Then, suddenly, we arrived at the crater at a spot called Stella Point, just as the sun began to rise. To one side was the ice-filled caldera of Kibo, to the other the Great Rift Valley far below. Uhuru Peak is another two hundred meters or so from Stella Rim on a flat trail that follows the rim. I didn't make it to Uhuru, as I didn't feel well. Nonetheless, I felt a huge sense of achievement that I made it to the rim, that I'd proven to myself that I could mentally and physically do it."

ALLY BURNETT is the founder of Burnett & Green Travel (www.burnettandgreentravel .com), an independent travel consultancy based in Florida and Colorado. Ally worked for Abercrombie & Kent for 10 years developing the company's European, Caribbean and Latin America portfolios. After a stint as Director of Sales & Marketing Europe for Oberoi Hotels, she returned to Cox & Kings, working as General Manager in the company's Tampa, Florida office before starting her own company with her new husband. Ally is a keen adventurer and has climbed Mount Kinabalu in Borneo, trekked to the base of Chomolhari in Bhutan, sailed in the Mediterranean and white water rafted the Orange River in South Africa. She enjoys skiing, hiking, horse riding, and sailing, as well as spending time indoors with a good book and a glass of wine.

If You Go

▶ **Getting There:** Climbers fly to Kilimanjaro International Airport near Arusha, Tanzania, which is served by KLM (800-225-2525; www.klm.com).

▶ **Best Time to Visit:** Kilimanjaro can be climbed most of the year. December through February generally promise warm, dry weather. The Tanzania National Parks Web site (www.tanzaniaparks.com) provides background information.

▶ **Accommodations:** The Tanzania Tourist Board Web site (tanzaniatouristboard.com) lists lodging options in Moshi or Arusha.

▶ **Guides/Outfitters:** Many outfitters lead climbs to Uhuru Peak. Cox and Kings (800-999-1758; www.coxandkingsusa.com) specializes in comfortable treks to the peak.

DESTINATION

40

GREAT SMOKY MOUNTAINS
NATIONAL PARK

RECOMMENDED BY **Heather Sable**

Heather Sable's quest to hike the Appalachian Trail (AT) began a few miles east of the trail in Baltimore, a city perhaps better known for crab festivals and Edgar Allan Poe than intense physical exercise.

"When I was in high school, I picked up a book called *The Baltimore Trail Book*," Heather began. "It listed day hikes in the area, and a couple of overnights—including one called the Appalachian Trail. I'd seen pictures of people backpacking in magazines and it intrigued me, so I talked a friend into going, bought a five-dollar backpack at a garage sale and some canned food and set a date. My parents dropped us at a trailhead near Route 70 in Frederick, Maryland, and off we went. Near Harper's Ferry, West Virginia, we came upon two guys, one with long hair and a long beard. Speaking to these fellows, I learned that the AT stretched from Georgia to Maine—I'd thought it was a three-day hike near Baltimore! I decided that hiking the trail was something I'd do before I died.

"One of my best qualities is that if I say I'm going to do something, I'm going to do it. Even if it takes some time. My hike was put off for nearly eight years. First I had to finish high school, then college, then put my education to work. But I planned that after a few years in the workforce, I'd take six months off to do the trail. In the meantime, I began slowly accumulating the equipment I'd need (largely through holiday and birthday gifts from friends and relatives) and spoke to people who'd completed the trail. Many go onto the trail with the attitude that they're going to be inspired to know what to do with the rest of their lives. I didn't do it to learn who I was or what I was. Instead, I hoped to understand what it was to live simply and to complete a large challenge."

More than seventy miles of the Appalachian Trail run through Great Smoky Mountains National Park, which straddles 800 square miles along the border of western North

Carolina and southeastern Tennessee. For through-hikers, the stretch through the park represents several high points. "By the time you reach the Smokies," Heather continued, "you're still pretty early into the hike, but some of the people who realize they're not cut out for this experience have been weeded out. You're beginning to develop some close friendships, and getting your trail names. I should mention that no one goes by their given name on the AT. Everyone is given a trail name, so you start a new life on the trail, leaving your background behind. For 99 percent of the people I hiked with, I still don't know their real names! In the Smokies, you're beginning to get into some of the first rugged terrain of the hike. You feel it, as you're not in great shape yet, so it's a physical as well as a mental challenge. You reach the highest elevation of the whole AT in the Smokies, at Clingman's Dome (6,625 feet on the trail; 6,643 at the summit). There's a lot of fine ridge hiking in the park, which is a nice break from going up and down hills. You can watch the clouds pass from one side of a ridge to the other—that is, if the ridges weren't cloaked in morning fog. The fog could be so thick at times that you couldn't see the person right in front of you. Though it blocked some views, it gave the surroundings a mystical feeling." (The fog that often visits the park in the morning and after a rainstorm gave it its name, as it appeared like plumes of smoke to early visitors.)

Great Smoky Mountains National Park is America's most popular national park, seeing upward of 9,000,000 visitors a year. The park hosts a tremendous diversity of plants and animals, thanks to its elevation diversity (from 875 to 6,643 feet) and ample rainfall; species common to the southern United States find suitable habitat in the lower elevations of the park, while species common in the northern states thrive in higher elevations. Some come to see one of the park's 1,200 black bears, a symbol of wildness in the increasingly populated Southeast. Many come for the hiking. Great Smoky Mountains National Park boasts 850 miles of trails and unpaved roads, including 150 "official" trails—a splendid variety of day hikes and overnighters. Many backpackers who hope to get a taste of the AT will come to hike a portion or all of the seventy miles of the route that run through the park, but this provides only a glimpse of the Smokies' possibilities. Whether you're seeking wildflowers, waterfalls, or old-growth forest, the park can deliver.

"I have some very strong memories of the Smoky Mountains section of the trail," Heather reminisced. "The shelters stood out for me. Many along the AT are very basic— just lean-tos, really, with a roof and three sides. In Great Smoky Mountain National Park, there's a collection of old stone structures, some with a wood-burning fireplace and a

DESTINATION

41

door that closes. It was a wonderful feeling to come off a long day on the trail to the smell of a roaring fire and the promise of warmth and camaraderie. I also recall reaching Newfound Gap, where the trail crosses from Tennessee into North Carolina. On many stretches of the AT, the trail passes close to towns fairly frequently. That's not the case for the section in the Smokies, which is more remote. An exception to this rule is Newfound Gap, which is a spot where a major road crosses the trail. The flush toilets and pavement and a parking lot filled with cars were a culture shock. I recall hiking up to the next shelter with a strong scent of clothing detergent in my nostrils, something I would've never noticed at home."

HEATHER SABLE is a trail programs manager at the American Hiking Society, where she spearheads programs including National Trails Day® and National Trails Fund, and is editor of *American Hiker* magazine. A Baltimore native, Heather attended Florida Southern College in Lakeland, Florida, and graduated with a BA in advertising and public relations. Before joining the American Hiking Society, she worked on the agency side of the advertising industry for eight years. An Appalachian Trail through-hiker in 2003, Heather is an avid outdoors enthusiast and enjoys hiking, backpacking, kayaking, biking, and running.

If You Go

▶ **Getting There:** The western entrance of Great Smoky Mountains National Park is roughly forty-five miles from Knoxville (served by most major carriers); the eastern entrance is sixty miles from Asheville (served by Delta, Northwest, and U.S. Airways).
▶ **Best Time to Visit:** Hikers can find rewards in the Smoky Mountains throughout the year, though you'll likely find snow on the higher trails from December through March and high humidity in the summer months (at least at lower elevations).
▶ **Accommodations:** The Great Smoky Mountains National Park Web site (www.nps .gov/grsm) includes links to town chambers of commerce near the park.

BIG BEND NATIONAL PARK

RECOMMENDED BY **David Elkowitz**

A great river park. A classic desert park. And, somewhat surprisingly, a mountain park. This is Big Bend National Park, deep in the heart of West Texas.

"It's hard to characterize Big Bend," David Elkowitz began, "because there's such a diversity of habitats. As you drive in from the north entrance, you begin to see the southern end of the Rocky Mountains in the U.S., peaks that reach almost 8,000 feet. An hour's drive to the south, you have the Rio Grande, separating Texas from Mexico. Through much of the park, you have desert habitat, with creosote bush, mesquite, and many varieties of cactus. A number of avian flight paths intersect here, so there's excellent birding, including many rare species passing through. There's also a diversity of wildlife that ranges from black bear to javelina (which resemble small wild boars, though are a quite distinct species) to mountain lion. There are a number of fine day hikes and backcountry overnight hikes, even the chance to combine off-road driving or river rafting with backcountry exploration. If there's a unifying element to the many sides of Big Bend, I'd say it's that they're all wild, remote, and beautiful."

"Everything's bigger in Texas," as the old saw goes, and this aphorism certainly speaks to the grand open spaces of Big Bend. The park takes in more than 800,000 acres, extending north from the point where the Rio Grande turns to the northeast before its long, meandering southeastern course to the Gulf of Mexico; the turn gives the park its name. (A few of the early scenes in the Coen brothers' film *No Country for Old Men* give a great sense of the Big Bend region's landscape, particularly the antelope-hunting sequence.) The river has carved several spectacular canyons from the limestone in this section, including Santa Elena, Mariscal, and Boquillas. The riparian zone along the Rio Grande provides critical habitat for a variety of plant and animal life. Much of the midsec-

tion of the park is given over to desert terrain. The Chisos Mountains dominate the northern side of the park, rising abruptly, some 5,000 feet from the desert. Thanks to their elevation, the Chisos attract a bit more moisture than the surrounding environs, and support different flora than is found in other parts of the park, including aspen, Arizona cypress, ponderosa pine, and madrone. The elevation also makes for cooler temperatures, and the Chisos region attracts many of Big Bend's biped visitors who are leery of the desert heat.

Most national parks, by their very nature, are a bit off the grid. Perhaps no park in the Lower Forty-eight is further afield than Big Bend—the nearest airport with commercial flights is in Midland-Odessa, 235 miles to the northeast. Most visitors who make the effort to come this far stay for a while, and there are plenty of fine hikes to keep walkers happy. A few of Dave's favorite day hikes are the Lost Mine, Window, Mule Ears Spring, and South Rim trails. "For the modest amount of effort it takes—almost five miles round-trip—Lost Mine in the Chisos gives you a tremendous view out over the park into Mexico—and the first southern vantage point is only a mile up the trail. The Window Trail, also in the Chisos, showcases a little more variety in terms of ecosystems. It starts in high country, going through scrub vegetation with great mountain views, and slowly drops down into a shady canyon. At the bottom of the trail is the Window, a slot in the canyon where there's a drop-off of 200 feet; the whole Chiso Basin drains through here. Mule Ears Spring, on the west side of the park, brings you across several arroyos to the spring, which resembles a Japanese garden against the dry surroundings. The 'mule ears' are a pair of peaks just behind that lead you to this little oasis." If you want to stretch your legs a bit more, the twelve-mile South Rim trail (and the southern edge of the Chisos) takes you 2,000-plus feet above the desert floor, offering what David considers to be one of the best views in Texas.

The Outer Mountain Loop is the signature multiday circuit at Big Bend, accentuating both the remoteness and the ecosystem variety of the park. Lack of water, lack of shade, and almost constant uphills and downhills make this thirty-miler through the Sierra Quemada ("burnt mountains") extremely rigorous; in fact, hikers are warned to avoid the hike from May to early October, due to what park officials deem "the physical impossibility of being able to carry enough water." Even during milder months, hikers are strongly encouraged to cache water at two caching stations along the loop, which unites the Pinnacles, Boot Canyon, Juniper Canyon, Dodson, Blue Creek, and Laguna Meadows

OPPOSITE:
Hikers can find
some relief from
the desert heat
of Big Bend
in the Chisos
Mountains on
the northern side
of the park.

DESTINATION

42

trails. The reward is a tour de force of Big Bend, from the piñon-peppered woodlands of the Chisos to the austere beauty of the desert.

"One of the best-kept secrets about Big Bend is how uncrowded we are in the summer," David added. "Most of our visitors come in the winter, as people have a perception that it's just too hot here in the summer months. The reality is that in some parts of the park—especially the Chisos sections—the temperature is generally in the eighties. There are nice, gentle showers that keep things green, and lots of hummingbirds are around. Big Bend is a great place to be when the other national parks are crowded."

DAVID ELKOWITZ is the chief of interpretation (chief naturalist) at Big Bend National Park. He has been a National Park Service ranger since 1985, during which time he has served at six national parks, including southwestern parks such as Carlsbad Caverns, El Malpais, and Padre Island National Seashore. David is a graduate of the University of Connecticut with a Bachelor of Science degree in wildlife biology. He is a lifelong naturalist with special interest in ornithology and herpetology. David first visited Big Bend in 1979, and has hiked throughout the park extensively for more than twenty-five years.

If You Go

▶ **Getting There:** The airport nearest to Big Bend National Park is in Midland-Odessa, Texas (235 miles from park headquarters). Midland is served by Continental Airlines (800-523-3273; www.continental.com) and American Airlines (800-433-7300; www.aa.com).

▶ **Best Time to Visit:** Big Bend sees most of its visitors in the winter and early spring. The park is very uncrowded in the summer.

▶ **Guides/Outfitters:** Desert Sports (888-989-6900; www.desertsportstx.com) leads hiking trips in Big Bend and the surrounding region.

▶ **Accommodations:** The Chisos Mountains Lodge (877-386-4383; www.chisos mountainslodge.com) provides the only lodging available inside the park.

THE KANGSHUNG VALLEY

RECOMMENDED BY **Jim Sano**

Very few mountaineers will ever reach the summit of Mount Everest. A similarly exclusive group can boast that they've gazed upon the eastern face of the world's tallest peak from the exquisite Kangshung Valley.

"Everest Base Camp can see up to 20,000 trekkers a year, going up and down one trail on the Nepalese side of the mountain (the North Face)," Jim Sano began. "The views of Everest from Kala Patthar are wonderful, but the traffic at the height of the season can be like some of the busier sections of the John Muir Trail. I led the American Women's Everest expedition up the North Face in 1983 and attempted the Western Ridge—we made it up to 28,000 feet, and then a storm beat us back. From here, we could peer into Tibet. At the time, it was a forbidden fruit. But my interest was piqued. I always thought it would be fascinating to approach Everest from the east—the Kangshung Face. (Kangshung is the name given to the glacier that begins at the eastern foot of Everest.)

"Tibet slowly opened up to foreign visitors, and in 1996, I was finally able to trek into this vast wilderness. The trek to the Kangshung Valley, where mountaineers staged for their assaults on the East Face, gives you a real sense of the drama of the Himalaya. Once you leave the trailhead, there are no villages. You may come upon a few yak herders, but that's your only human contact. In all the years that my associates and I have led trips to the Kangshung Face, we've never seen another trekking group. We like to think of it as our own private Everest."

The Kangshung Face and its magnificent valleys—Kama, Kangshung, and Kharta—were first viewed by Westerners in 1921, during a British expedition (that included George Mallory) sent to explore possible climbing routes for Everest. Kangshung, with

DESTINATION

43

its hanging glaciers and snow slopes that threatened avalanches, did not seem a wise bet for these mountaineers, yet they reveled in the lushly flowered meadows of the valley. In the coming years, six Everest ascents were launched from the Rongbuk Valley to the north. Geographic Expeditions' unofficial historian, Tom Cole, has noted that "when the mountaineers tired of the Rongbuk's dry rocks, they would slip over a high pass discovered by Mallory and bask in the warmth and greenery of the eastern valleys." The valleys captured their imagination, as evidenced in this passage from Sir Francis Younghusband's *The Epic of Mount Everest* (Younghusband was a president of the Royal Geographic Society and chairman of the society's Mount Everest Committee):

> The Kama Valley . . . must be the most beautiful valley in the whole Himalaya. The beauty in the Kama Valley lay in this, that it came straight down from Mount Everest, which filled in all the upper part; that it ran directly under the mighty cliffs of Makalu, a mountain not 2,000 feet lower and even more beautiful than Everest; and that its fall was so rapid that while these two great peaks were in full view it had yet descended to altitudes where luxuriant vegetation was possible. . . . Right opposite the climbers as they [ascended toward the East Face] were the dazzling cliffs of Makalu and Chomolonzo dropping an almost sheer 10,000 feet into the valley below and now powdered white with fresh fallen snow—a spectacle of perhaps unequaled mountain glory.

The drive to reach the trailhead near the village of Kharta (and its namesake valley) provides an exhilarating preamble to the trek—sometimes at altitudes exceeding 17,000 feet. You'll pass the vast inland sea of Yamdrok Lake, the walled monastery of Palkhor Chiode, and cross Pang La (*la* is Tibetan for "pass"), which, on a clear day, exposes jaw-dropping views of the long crest of the Himalaya, from Makalu (27,817 feet) to Chomolonzo (also known as Everest, at 29,128 feet), and Lhotse (27,916 feet) to Gyachung Kang (25,980 feet), to Cho Oyu (26,714 feet), and, to the west, Shisha Pangma (26,286 feet). After meeting up with the Sherpas (who've been recruited from Nepal to accompany the expedition), your thirteen-day trek will begin. Yaks are retained to carry everything beyond the contents of your day pack. "As Himalayan treks go, this one is not particularly difficult," Jim continued. "Days are usually not long—five to six hours at the most—distances are not great, and by Tibetan standards, altitudes are not tremendous. Our greatest daily altitude gain is not much more than 2,500 feet."

DESTINATION

43

There are many defining moments of the trek to Kangshung Valley. One comes on day three, as you cross through Shao La (at 16,000+ feet) to Kama Valley. Here, the arid tundra of the Tibetan plateau gives way to a subtropical riot of flora, the stunning greens, golds, and reds of juniper, silver fir, mountain ash, and rhododendron. "As you cross the pass, you're surrounded by an amphitheater of big peaks, including Makalu and Chomolonzo," Jim described. "There's nearly 13,000 feet of verticality—the equivalent of three El Capitáns—resting right in front of you." Another comes a few days later, when you reach a spot called Sakyetang. From here, the verdant Kangshung Valley is exposed— along with staggering views of three of the world's five highest mountains. "You will search the world in vain for a more heart-stoppingly gorgeous spot," Jim added. The high camp, Pethang Ringmo, was established by George Mallory and G. H. Bullock on the expedition of 1921. From this sunny camp below the cliffs of Chomolonzo (separated from your tent by the mile-wide Kangshung Glacier), you'll have a few days to explore. One walk leads to a dramatic overlook of the East Face, called "Land's End," as only the glacier separates you from the Kangshung Wall. Another climb takes you to a summit northeast of Land's End, the high point of the trek at 19,000 feet.

Before descending to the Kharta Valley, there are a few more chances to drink in the wonders of Chomolungma. Perhaps most startling is the sunrise on day ten from a lakeside camp at 16,300 feet. "In a few intense moments," Jim recalled, "Everest and the whole panoply of peaks change from cold pewter to rose, to gold, to blinding white."

JIM SANO is the president of Geographic Expeditions, which organizes a diverse array of journeys to remote destinations, with a focus on complicated logistics and special-interest travel. Jim was formerly a park ranger and executive assistant to the superintendent at Yosemite National Park, where his duties included overseeing park-naturalist programs, participating in search-and-rescue operations, and coordinating several key elements of the Yosemite General Management Plan. He was the leader of the 1983 American Mount Everest Expedition, via Lho La and the West Ridge (which set the American women's altitude record); a coleader on the first guided ski-mountaineering trip to traverse South Georgia island in the sub-Antarctic; the leader of the first Western expedition to reach Gangkhar Puensum (then the highest unclimbed mountain in the world); the leader of several expeditions in the Nepalese Himalaya; and has extensively explored some of the world's most remote destinations. Jim currently serves on the

National Board of the Trust for Public Land. He was the founding president of the Mono Lake Foundation, a founding director of the Natural Step and the Yosemite Restoration Trust, and a National Council member of the World Wildlife Fund.

If You Go

▶ **Getting There:** Expeditions to Kangshung Valley begin in Kathmandu, Nepal, which is generally reached via Hong Kong or Bangkok. Kathmandu is served by many international carriers, including China Airlines (800-227-5118 ; www.china-airlines.com).

▶ **Best Time to Visit:** Trips generally depart in mid-May or late September.

▶ **Guides/Outfitters:** Geographic Expeditions (800-777-8183; www.geoex.com) has led a number of successful trips to Kangshung Valley, and handles all logistics for your adventure.

DESTINATION

43

LHASA

RECOMMENDED BY **John Ackerly**

"As a passionate hiker, I used to love going to Tibet," John Ackerly declared, "not just for the wonderful mountains, but to be in a place where hiking and trekking is such a part of the national culture. Much of Tibetans' trekking has a deep spiritual component—they walk as part of a pilgrimage. The destination for many pilgrims is Lhasa."

For devout Buddhists and adventurers alike, Lhasa (which translates into English as "country of the gods") has long held a revered place in the imagination. The city, the capital of the Tibet Autonomous Region, rests in a valley on the north bank of the Lhasa River at an elevation of nearly 12,000 feet. Lhasa was established in the seventh century AD, and by the 1500s had risen to prominence as the center of Tibetan Buddhism and the seat of government. It was the traditional home of the Dalai Lama, Tibet's secular and religious head, until the fourteenth (current) Dalai Lama fled Lhasa for India in 1959, soon after the start of the Chinese occupation of the country. (The Dalai Lama continues to live in exile in Dharamsala in northern India, where he presides over the Tibetan government-in-exile.) Some of Tibetan Buddhism's most sacred temples and monasteries are in Lhasa, including the Potala, the palace of the Dalai Lama, which has an imprint on the city's landscape that rivals that of the surrounding massifs.

For many Tibetan trekkers, Lhasa may be a staging area for an expedition or a one-day stopover on a larger tour. John has come to see it as a hiking destination itself. "All of the monasteries and temples have circumambulation paths where devotees perform *kora*—a form of prayer or meditation. Some of the faithful chant or spin while circling the sacred structure, others are quietly contemplative. During some of my early visits to Tibet, I discovered that hiking up to the monasteries was a great workout, and provided wonderful views of the city below, as well as of the surrounding mountains. Some of the

OPPOSITE:
A view of the
imposing Potala
Palace, Lhasa's
most dramatic
manmade
landmark.

DESTINATION

44

193

circumambulations took just an hour door-to-door, others were a half-day or more. They all provided a chance to experience an important aspect of Tibetan culture." How John happened to discover the hiking possibilities in the hills above Lhasa is worth further explanation. "Many people in the international community who were concerned about humanrights violations in Tibet insisted that there were prisons around Lhasa," John continued, "but there was some skepticism as well. And back in 1987, no photos of the prisons existed. One of the reasons I first traveled there was to get some photos that would prove the prisons' existence. I started hiking the hills so I could get a better idea of where they were located and figure out the best angles for shooting pictures. Someone pointed out that going out into the hills as a hiker would provide a good cover if the authorities asked what I was up to. After all, the scenery gives you a pretty good reason to be hiking around."

You needn't wander more than a few blocks from downtown Lhasa to find your first pilgrimage walk, the Lingkor. This circumambulation—around the perimeter of the old (and holy) city of Lhasa—can begin near the Potala. It takes you past the Lukhang (temple of the serpent spirits), the blue visage of Menlha (the Medicine Buddha) on the side of Chakpori hill, and concludes near Norbulingka, which was constructed in the mid-1700s by the seventh and eighth Dalai Lamas, and used as a summer retreat. Once your legs are stretched a bit and your lungs acclimatized to the altitude, you can tackle the Sera Monastery circuit, a bit north of Lhasa. This first *kora* here circles the complex of temples and colleges within the monastery, and continues past a series of special rocks that pilgrims touch or circle, brightly colored rock paintings, and resident dogs. (Writer Gary McCue points out that some Tibetans believe these dogs are fallen monks; food offerings for the canines are encouraged.) Next, you can head further uphill past Choding Gon Temple to the Sera Tse Hermitage, set in a grove of trees directly above the monastery. Views across the Lhasa Valley from the hermitage are inspiring.

One of John's most memorable experiences around Lhasa came at a nunnery called Michungri, a large white-washed structure a few miles north of the city. "My sense is that hardly anyone goes up to Michungri," John said. "It's a stiff hike up a steep hill, and I expect that this loop may only get a few dozen tourists a year. I went up there with my wife once, and we were treated to tea. The nuns were very excited that we were there, and interested in us as Americans; Tibetans generally love the American people. I was also struck by how playful they were, especially knowing the hardships they'd endured at the hands of the Chinese government. We spent hours 'talking' with our hands. We almost spent the night up at Michungri, but it was ultimately decided that having outsiders staying over might be too politically sensitive. The nuns fed us a meal in their lofty citadel, high above Lhasa. You feel like you're very far away from town, though it's only a few miles."

John has not visited Tibet since 2000. He's unable to get a visa, due to his efforts to document human rights abuses there. "I knew that one of the hazards of my job with the International Campaign for Tibet was that I might be barred from going to Tibet. But each time I went, I felt blessed. Hopefully I will one day be able to return with my young son."

JOHN ACKERLY is president of the Alliance for Green Heat, which promotes high-efficiency wood combustion as a carbon-neutral, sustainable, local, and affordable heating solution. He formerly served as the president of the International Campaign for Tibet (ICT). He has written many reports on Tibet, including: "Forbidden Freedom: Beijing's Control of Religion in Tibet," "The Suppression of a People: Accounts of Torture and Imprisonment in Tibet," "Nuclear Tibet: Nuclear Weapons and Nuclear Waste on the Tibetan Plateau," "A Season to Purge: Religious Repression in Tibet," and "Jampa: The Story of Racism in Tibet." He has worked closely with the U.S. Congress and United Nations bodies to address the crisis in Tibet and has conducted five fact-finding trips to investigate conditions. John attended Dartmouth College and the Washington College of Law. Prior to joining ICT, John practiced civil-rights law in a private firm in Mississippi.

If You Go

▶ **Getting There:** Lhasa, Tibet, is reached via Beijing and Chengdu, China, via China Airlines (800-227-5118 ; www.china-airlines.com).

▶ **Best Time to Visit:** Despite its high altitude, Lhasa has clement weather much of the year. You can enjoy the walks described above from April through October. Gary McCue's book, *Trekking in Tibet*, offers directions to many of the day hikes around Lhasa.

▶ **Accommodations:** The Lhasa Hotel (+86 0891 6824509; www.lhasahotel.com.cn) was formerly operated as a Holiday Inn, and will meet most travelers' standards.

DESTINATION

44

THE LYCIAN COAST

RECOMMENDED BY **Tricia Dowhan**

"To me, Turkey is a fascinating destination," Tricia Dowhan began. "From a historical perspective, there are vestiges of so many important cultures—Roman, Byzantine, Ottoman. There's such a wealth of national treasures, from Roman aqueducts and amphitheaters to sites that have been recounted in mythology. You can walk (or swim) right among sarcophagi dating back thousands of years. There's no graffiti on these artifacts; many times, there are not even other people around. You feel as though you're walking in a living museum. Even if you're not a history buff, you're in awe of the natural beauty of the place, and the incredible access to historic sites. Walking along the coast is a rich sensory experience. There are the blues and greens of the sea, the bright blue sky, the greens of the pine forests, and the air is perfumed with lavender, wild mint, thyme, and pine."

OPPOSITE: The Oludeniz Lagoon along Turkey's Lycian Coast is one of the Mediterranean's most picturesque coves.

Turkey, perhaps more than any nation in the world, truly straddles the borders of East and West. It's an Islamic nation, but is democratic and aspires toward membership in the European Union. It borders Bulgaria and Greece to the west, but touches Georgia, Armenia, Naxcivan, Iran, Iraq, and Syria to the east and south; as one pundit has put it, Turkey is "a neighbor to the entire world." It's the clash and assimilation of very different cultures that makes Turkey such a fascinating tourist destination; that, and it's astonishingly beautiful and unspoiled southern coast. Turkey has more than 2,600 miles of coastline along its southern reaches, with the eastern third of the coast bordering on the Mediterranean Sea, the remainder bordering on the Aegean. Tricia's walking tour of Turkey took her along the Mediterranean section, sometimes called the Blue, Turquoise, or Lycian Coast. It's a remarkable stretch of terrain, indented with countless bays often graced with pine forests. At times, it seems more like Maine than the Mediterranean.

DESTINATION

45

The adventure begins in Antalya, a walled port city that dates back to the second century BC. The minarets poking up along the skyline and the call of the muezzin seem somehow out of place against the Mediterranean, but add a sense of mystery to the city, which was inhabited in turn by Romans, Byzantines, and Seljuks before the Ottomans took control. Leaving Antalya, you'll travel west along the coast by coach or *gulet* (the traditional Turkish sailing craft), stopping for walks along the way. Most of the walks highlight historical aspects of the Lycian Coast. One of Tricia's favorites unfolds around Mount Olympos (not to be confused with Mount Olympus in Greece; some twenty mountains were named some version of Olympus in classical literature!) "You take a gondola ride to the summit of the mountain, which sits at an elevation of 7,700 feet. From here—the spot where, according to Homer, Poseidon watched Odysseus sailing into the distance and conjured up the storm that kept him at sea for ten years—you can enjoy sweeping views of the coastline with its jagged cliffs and stands of Aleppo pines.

"After returning to the base of the mountain, you start on a coastal walk that leads to the ancient ruins at Phaselis, a former Roman port town set on three pine-shaded coves. When I last did the trip, we took our lunch with a local family in the town of Ulupinar, just beyond Phaselis. The mother made a wonderful meal of *katmer*, rolling flatbread dough out on a wide metal sheet over a fire and filling it with herbs, local onions, cheese, and spices. After lunch, my group set out on a path that led gradually downhill, crossed a stream, and then climbed uphill to another mythological site—the eternal flames of Chimera. It was here, in *The Iliad*, that the Greek hero Bellerophon defeated the Chimera—a part-lion, part-goat, part-dragon monster—with the help of his steed, Pegasus. If you're expecting grandiose flames, you'll be disappointed—but there are flames, thanks to natural gas that results from seismic activity in the area. Again, it's wonderful to come face-to-face with history, and to reconcile reality and mythology."

Moving along the coast, there are ample opportunities to take in historic sites and drink in local culture. "There are so many beautiful towns along the Lycian Coast," Tricia observed. "Places like Kaş, Kalkan, and Fethiye, where you can pop into a local café, have a coffee and watch the fishermen come in with their catch. It's amazing that this coastline has remained so undiscovered." At one point, your *gulet* reaches Ölüdeniz Lagoon, renowned in Turkey as the "jewel of the Mediterranean." From here, you embark on a spectacular walk along Aleppo pine–shaded headlands to the Greek ghost town of

Kayaköy. "The Greeks who once lived here were forced to return to their native country in the 1920s as part of the mass population exchanges between Greece and Turkey," Tricia explained. "The 600 stone houses they once occupied have been left vacant, as the local Turkish people were concerned that the houses might be haunted by evil spirits."

A moment that defined Tricia's walking tour of the Lycian Coast came near the ancient town of Simena (today known as Kaleköy). "I was walking from Skyrock Bay up toward Simena, where a crusader castle rests on the hilltop above the village," she recalled. "The trail takes you through copses of age-old olive trees, carob groves, and vivid green fields. I was hardly paying attention to the immediate scenery, as I was very excited to get to the castle—the walls of the compound are littered with dozens of Roman sarcophagi from the first century, adorned with ornate carvings. Crossing a field, I came upon a young man and his son, who was about four years old. They were with a lamb they had just helped deliver. Up the hill was the ancient Roman fortress, but here at my feet was contemporary life unfolding—though a slice of life that's been repeated for thousands of years. I was so taken with this juxtaposition that I nearly forgot about the sarcophagi."

TRICIA DOWHAN is a senior manager at Country Walkers, which leads walking tours around the world. Her passion for foreign languages—she is fluent in French and Italian—has led to educational and professional pursuits in both France and Italy. She has worked in the travel industry for almost 20 years; when not creating trips of a lifetime, she can often be found exploring exotic parts of the globe with her husband and son.

If You Go

▶ **Getting There:** The circuit begins in Antalya, Turkey, and ends near Dalaman. Both cities are served from Istanbul on Turkish Airlines (800-874-8875; www.turkishairlines.com).
▶ **Best Time to Visit:** The Lycian Coast has a Mediterranean climate, with the promise of sun from April to October. Early fall can be particularly pleasant.
▶ **Accommodations:** The Turkish Department of Culture and Tourism (212-687-2194; www.tourismturkey.org) provides an overview of lodging options.
▶ **Guides/Outfitters:** A number of outfitters lead walking tours of the Lycian Coast, including Country Walkers (800-464-9255; www.countrywalkers.com).

DESTINATION

45

THE LONG TRAIL

RECOMMENDED BY **Ben Rose**

When asked what makes Vermont's Long Trail special, Ben Rose was succinct: "There are not many other places where you can walk from one end of a state to another without seeing anything ugly."

The Long Trail stretches 273 miles, from Vermont's southern boundary with Massachusetts (just north of Williamstown) to the Québec border near the town of Troy. The trail follows the main ridgeline of the Green Mountains, crossing Vermont's highest peaks along the way. "The organizing geographic principle was simple," Ben explained. "Keep as much of Vermont below your feet as possible."

Even the most casual hiker knows something of the Appalachian Trail (AT), but they may not realize that 150 miles of the AT pass through the Green Mountain State—and that the Long Trail is the oldest long-distance hiking path in the United States and was actually the inspiration for the AT. (For the first hundred miles of the AT in southern Vermont, it's conjoined with the Long Trail. It veers east at a spot called Maine Junction; Long Trail hikers will tell you that the AT is just another side walk off the Long Trail!) The Long Trail was conceived by a schoolteacher named James P. Taylor and was brought into being by a group of Vermont citizens who formed an organization called the Green Mountain Club in 1910. Ben picked up the Long Trail's creation story: "Taylor liked to take his students on hikes in the mountains, and thought it would be great if the trails were connected. He assembled a group of like-minded men in Burlington [the state's largest city] to discuss this and the larger notion of how the mountains could play a bigger role in the lives of Vermonters, while acting as an attraction for tourists. This was a very new way of thinking, as mountains weren't much celebrated at this time; instead, they were viewed as cold, dark, and brooding impediments to commerce and transport, rather than

OPPOSITE:
The Long Trail stretches the entire length of Vermont, and was the inspiration for the Appalachian Trail.

DESTINATION

46

as potential revenue generators. Taylor was talking about ecotourism before the term had been created."

James P. Taylor's and the Green Mountain Club's vision took hold, and by 1930, the last section of trail had been cut, connecting Vermont with the Canadian border. Since that time, the Green Mountain Club has been inextricably linked with the wellbeing of the Long Trail. The club relies upon more than 800 volunteers (through fourteen local chapters) to maintain the trail and sixty-six shelters along the way. The survival of the trail is an annual miracle of volunteerism. The Vermont legislature has recognized the Green Mountain Club as an official caretaker of the trail. Speaking of legislature, Ben felt it important to clarify the Long Trail's role in Vermont politics. "Though many may now picture Vermont as a fairly liberal state, the state was considered the most conservative in the nation during much of the 20th century. Vermont was the only state never to vote for FDR. Vermonters did not like the New Deal, in part because of a proposed New Deal initiative called the Green Mountain Parkway, which would have been a high-elevation scenic road that would have essentially paved over parts of the Long Trail. In an odd turn of events, the Green Mountain Club, which staunchly opposed the road, found itself battling its founder, James P. Taylor, who had gone on to be the first chief executive officer of the chamber of commerce of Vermont."

Vermonters, incidentally, voted down the Green Mountain Parkway. "The Long Trail is a romantic thing to have on the landscape," Ben added. "Even those residents who don't hike can look up at the ridgeline and know that there's a public footpath up there, and feel a connection."

"Imposing" may not be the first word that comes to mind when attempting to describe the Green Mountains. The highest point in the chain, Mount Mansfield, tops out at 4,393 feet, and only four other mountains eclipse 4,000 feet. To someone more accustomed to the crenellated peaks of the Rockies or Alps, the Greens may seem more like hills in places, gently rolling ones at that. But appearances can be misleading. "The Long Trail is very much a backcountry hiking experience," Ben continued. "While there may not be any especially tall summits, I've heard many say that it's as tough as any trail they've been on, with roots, rocks, and few switchbacks to ease steep inclines—and, Vermont natives say that they have five seasons—winter, spring, summer, fall, and mud." Ben explained the spring phenomenon: "You have snow melting, rain falling, and the trees are not yet budding to absorb the water. You're left with mud. The state actually closes portions of the trail around Mount Mansfield from April 15 to Memorial Day. Somewhere along the way, proponents of the Long Trail began calling it a 'footpath in the wilderness.' Some have joked that in the spring, it's a 'foot bath in the wilderness.'"

Muddy or not, the Long Trail exposes the varied terrain of Vermont's largely unspoiled forests, passing pristine ponds, alpine bogs, and rushing streams, and offering well-earned views when you exit what Ben calls "the Green Tunnel" and come out upon a ridge or summit. "The mountains get more rugged as you get north," Ben explained. "For that reason, most through hikers start in the south, so they can get warmed up. The southern portions have some wonderful water features—Stratton Pond may be the most beautiful swimming spot on the entire Appalachian Trail. Little Rock Pond and Griffith Lake are not far behind. It's a treat to camp near the lakes and hear the loons. Thanks to the short distance between shelters, through-hikers have more choice regarding the nature of their social experience. If you want to hang back or push ahead to get with some different folks, you have that option without having to hike an extra-long distance. About 200 people complete the Long Trail each year, though some of those folks have chipped away a few miles a year for twenty years."

Most would say that the Long Trail's most iconic day hike leads to Camel's Hump, on the northern section of the trail, roughly twenty-five miles southeast of Burlington. Camel's Hump, as its name implies, has a unique shape, and is quite distinctive from other peaks in the Greens. A popular route is to take the Monroe Trail from the east to the Long Trail, then on up to the summit. "Several hundred feet of Camel's Hump (4,083 feet) are above tree line," Ben explained, "and this area—along with portions of Mount Mansfield and Mount Abraham comprises Vermont's alpine zones. Here you'll find plants that are unlike anything else in Vermont; similar to the species found 1,500 miles north in Labrador. Hikers are required to stay on the trail here to protect the flora.

"There's a unique light when you're on the exposed ridgeline on Mount Mansfield or Camel's Hump in the late afternoon. The sun slants over the Adirondacks to the west at a certain angle, and the Champlain Valley and Lake Champlain are lit up before you. I can always summon this image, wherever I am."

BEN ROSE has been executive director of the Green Mountain Club since 1998. In 1984, he co-founded the Catamount Trail Association; the Catamount Trail is a cross-country ski trail the length of Vermont, parallel to the Long Trail. He holds a BA from

DESTINATION

46

Yale University and an MS from the University of Vermont's School of Natural Resources. He served two terms in the Vermont House of Representatives, from 1995–1998. Ben is a Justice of the Peace in Williston, Vermont, where he lives with his wife, Lori Fisher, and their teenaged son and daughter. During Williston's annual Fourth of July parade, Ben is Commander of the Sue Pasco Memorial Williston Precision Lawn Chair March and Drill Team.

If You Go

▶ **Getting There:** The northern and central parts of the Long Trail are easily reached from Burlington, Vermont, which is served by a number of airlines, including Continental (800-523-3273; www.continental.com), Delta (800-221-1212; www.delta.com) and United (800-864-8331; www.united.com). The closest major airport to the southern section is Hartford, Connecticut, which is served by many carriers.

▶ **Best Time to Visit:** Visitors arriving from June through September will likely avoid snow and mud . . . though there will be bugs. The Green Mountain Club (802-244-7037; www.greenmountainclub.org) can provide up-to-date conditions. The club also publishes several trail guides and maps for the Long Trail.

▶ **Accommodations:** The Vermont Department of Tourism (800-837-6668; www.travel vermont.com) highlights lodging options all along the Long Trail.

OLYMPIC NATIONAL PARK

RECOMMENDED BY **Chiggers Stokes**

Olympic National Park rests on the northwestern edge of the continental United States, on a wind- and rain-swept peninsula that's a study in gray, green, and occasionally blue. "Many say that Olympic National Park is three parks in one," began Chiggers Stokes. "First, it's a park for arboreal resources. The river valleys of the park have a remnant of what was once the greatest temperate rainforest in the world. It's a museum piece for trees, holding the 'biggest tree' found anywhere for a variety of species. Olympic National Park also boasts the largest coastal wilderness in the Lower Forty-eight—more than seventy miles of coastline, with very limited access points. Toward the eastern side of the park, there's wonderful high country. Despite its modest elevation (the highest peak in the Olympic range, Mount Olympus, tops out at 7,829 feet), the Olympics are home to a number of glaciers.

"The thing that's most special to me about Olympic National Park is the opportunity for solitude. The park has almost one million acres, and 95 percent of that land is designated wilderness. No roads cut through the middle of the park, and though there are more than two million annual visitors, most stay close to Lake Crescent. With nearly 600 miles of trails, it's fairly easy to find magnificent country to hike through without being shoulder-to-shoulder with fellow enthusiasts, so you can experience nature without the madding crowd."

If there's a defining feature of Olympic National Park, it is water: the 135 inches of rain that fall on average in the Hoh River Basin and the more than fifty feet of snow that accumulate on Mount Olympus; the 3,000 miles of rivers and creeks that radiate from the park's central mountains, hosting healthy runs of salmon and steelhead trout and acting as a circulatory system for the park's varied ecosystems; the glaciers that helped form

DESTINATION

those mountains; and, finally, the Pacific, which delivers the massive weather fronts to the Olympic Peninsula in the first place. The most celebrated beneficiaries of all this water are the rainforests, and a hike up any of the river valleys on the west side of the park—the Quinault, Queets, Ho, and Bogachiel—will likely redefine your idea of "big tree." Sitka spruce and western hemlock dominate the landscape, but western red cedar, Douglas fir, and Engelmann spruce, among other conifers, are also present. Some of the largest specimens can approach sixty or seventy feet in circumference, and reach heights of more than 250 feet. Almost as impressive are the mosses, ferns, and lichens that spring from the trunks of these giants. Even in the less-than-bright light that's the norm most of the year, the tangles of green on display are so varied that they'd make the color-namers at Sherwin Williams jump for joy. (Wandering through the rainforests, be on the lookout for Roosevelt elk, the largest of elk species. The park is home to the country's largest wild population of these ungulates, which can range from 600 to 1,000 pounds.)

"The backpacking trip I'd recommend to get a great taste of some of the diversity of Olympic National Park would you take in toward the center of the park along the Sol Duc River and back out along the Hoh River," Chiggers continued. "You get a subalpine experience at the beginning of the hike as you head up toward Deer Lake. If the weather cooperates a little, you'll get beautiful views of Mount Olympus. From Deer Lake, I'd head to Bogachiel Peak and Hoh Lake, and then drop down to the Hoh, where you'll get the classic rainforest experience. Coming down from Bogachiel Peak to the Hoh, you descend from an elevation of more than a mile high to 600 feet over the course of thirty-six switchbacks."

There are several walks that allow you to take in the grandeur of the Olympic Peninsula's isolated coast. "You can drive to within a hundred yards of Rialto Beach, and walk a mile and a half up the beach to a spot called Hole in the Wall," Chiggers said. "It's a rock monolith with a tunnel punched through. This stretch of beach is a great spot to watch the waves crashing during bad weather, especially in the winter. If you're interested in a longer trip, you can take the North Coast Route from Ozette Trailhead in the north and hike south to Rialto Beach. It's twenty miles, a three- or four-day walk. One of my favorite places to take visitors is Second Beach, just a few miles south of Rialto Beach. For the amount of time you walk to get there, it's one of the best investments for scenic quality that you can make in the park as a hiker. It's only three quarters of a mile to get out to the beach, and there's a spectacular seascape on either end. To the north, there's an arch

OPPOSITE:
Olympic
National Park
offers brilliant,
unspoiled coastal
terrain, as well
as unmatched
old-growth forests.

DESTINATION

47

that's frequently featured on calendars. At the south end, there's an island that has a tunnel running through it, like a blowhole. There are sea caves, sea stacks—remnants of ancient volcanic activity. You'll often come upon seals and bald eagles." In March and April and again in October, it's possible to watch gray-whale migrations from Second Beach. Camping is allowed, but like at other sites along the coast, you'll need bear barrels for your food—not to protect it from bears, but to ward off raccoons. It's also prudent to take note of tidal flows, as during abnormally high tides, portions of the trail adjoining the beach may be more waterlogged than usual.

If you happen to visit Olympic National Park in the fall, you'll want to set aside an hour or two from the trail to take in one of nature's great spectacles—the sight of salmon leaping falls to reach their spawning grounds. Coho (sometimes called silver) salmon return to several rivers in the park in September and October, and there are several modest falls on the Hoko River (on the east side of the park) and the Sol Duc (near the center of the park) that are good bets for fish viewing, in season. While you're visiting the Sol Duc, you may consider a visit to the Sol Duc Hot Springs Resort. Here, for a modest fee, you can soak in a tiled pool of pleasantly heated mineral water. Do-it-yourselfers may prefer Olympic Hot Springs, a natural set of pools that sit a modest two-mile hike up the Boulder Creek Trail.

Even if you think you've had enough water after tramping around Olympic National Park, the hot springs may change your mind.

CHIGGERS STOKES was hired by the National Park Service as a resource educator and worked at the Chesapeake and Ohio National Historic Park for several years before becoming a river-safety technician on the Potomac River. He transferred to Olympic National Park in 1977, where he worked as a protection ranger until retiring on April 1, 2000. Since 1978, he has lived on a portion of the "Flying S" homestead (just outside Olympic National Park) settled by German immigrant Otto Siegfried before the turn of the twentieth century. In 1982, he electrified the property by a microhydroelectric scheme on Hemp Hill Creek, and writes by the lights and power from this alternative-energy project. *Nineteen Hundred and Ninety-Two* is Chiggers's first novel, written in 1991. *Between Forks and Alpha Centauri* is his second novel, written in 1997.

| If You Go |

▶ **Getting There:** The closest major airport is SeaTac, which is served by most major carriers; it's roughly three hours' drive to the park welcome center in Port Angeles. Kenmore Air (866-435-9524; www.kenmoreair.com) offers regular air-shuttle service from Seattle to Port Angeles.

▶ **Best Time to Visit:** Olympic National Park is situated in a temperate rainforest, and it can rain anytime. Nonetheless, July, August, and September are the driest months, with pleasant temperatures. Snow is generally gone from the high country by late June. The Olympic National Park Web site (www.nps.gov/olym) details backcountry guidelines and seasonal weather conditions.

▶ **Accommodations:** There are several lodging options within the park, including Log Cabin Resort (360-928-3325; www.logcabinresort.net), Lake Crescent Lodge (360-928-3211; www.lakecrescentlodge.com), Sol Duc Hot Springs Resort (866-476-5382; www.visitsolduc.com) and Kalaloch Lodge (866-525-2562; www.visitkalaloch.com). The Olympic Peninsula Tourist Commission (www.olympicpeninsula.org) highlights lodging options outside the park.

DESTINATION

47

NORTH CASCADES NATIONAL PARK

RECOMMENDED BY **Michael Lanza**

"The more difficult the access to a national park or hiking region, the fewer people you're going to find there," began Michael Lanza. "That's one of the great appeals of the North Cascades National Park. Though parts of the region are only three hours from Seattle—which is certainly a city with an outdoors orientation—there are many trails both inside and outside the national park where you don't see many, if any, people. From Stevens Pass and north, there's only one primary road that crosses the park, Highway 20. This road and the few other roads that run through are down in the valleys, and mostly hemmed in by trees. There are tremendous mountains and glaciers nearby, but there's no promise from the roadside of what's out there. You don't see what's waiting for you until you're out on the trail. It's not like driving through Jackson Hole, Wyoming, where there are iconic views of the Tetons from the get-go."

The more than two million acres that make up the North Cascades National Park are perhaps the largest wilderness area in the continental United States that you've never heard of. Extending from Lake Chelan in the south to the border with British Columbia in the north, it encompasses a large swath of the Cascade Mountains in between. One third of the area is contained in the North Cascades National Park Service Complex, which is divided into three units: North Cascades National Park and the Ross Lake and Lake Chelan National Recreation Areas. Nearly all of the park has been designated wilderness terrain within the Stephen Mather Wilderness. Adjoining wilderness areas (including Mount Baker Wilderness, Glacier Peak Wilderness, Pasayten Wilderness, and Chilliwack Lake, Skagit Valley, and Manning Provincial Parks in British Columbia) round out the offering. North Cascades National Park boasts more than 300 glaciers (700 in the North Cascades region), some 120 alpine lakes, and almost 400 miles of trails leading

OPPOSITE:

Cascade Pass
offers superb
vistas of volcanic
peaks and
hanging glaciers.

upward from old-growth Douglas-fir-and-hemlock-covered valley floors to rocky spires favored by mountaineers. Thanks to the light (often nonexistent) hand of man here, the North Cascades are home to fauna you wouldn't expect to find within a morning's drive of Seattle's Pike Place Market, including grizzly bears, gray wolves, lynx, moose, mountain goat, and even wolverine.

The challenges of hiking the North Cascades don't let up once you've managed to reach a trailhead. "Any trail that you get on, you're working hard from the get-go," Michael continued. "It's some of the most severe terrain in the world. It's not uncommon to have 6,000 feet of relief in three horizontal miles. The weather is difficult, too, frequently cool and rainy. And you won't find any big hotels or other comfortable amenities to retire to. All these facets of the North Cascades conspire to make it a relatively unknown place. There's not much here that's going to pull in anyone but the hard-core wilderness types. Of course, that's also a big part of its appeal. Once you get beyond the trailheads, you won't see many people."

North Cascades National Park and its adjoining wilderness area are managed for the plants and animals that live in the region, as well as for humans seeking a remote backpacking experience. That's not to say that there aren't some fine day hikes available. "From the North Cascades Scenic Byway [Highway 20], there are a number of short hikes that offer fabulous views," Michael added. "The most popular day hike is the Cascade Pass Trail. To reach the Cascade Pass Trail, you head up Cascade River Road at the little settlement of Marblemount. The road is paved at first and soon turns to gravel as it heads through the forest, then comes out at tree line. Here at the trailhead, there are enormous cliffs all around, hanging glaciers, waterfalls—it's one of the most fantastic trailheads I've ever seen." For those with limited time, Cascade Pass sums up everything the North Cascades have to offer. It's a fairly short and easy hike by North Cascades standards (about three and a half miles, with an elevation gain of 1,700 feet), winding upward through meadows to the pass, offering superb vistas of volcanic peaks (including Johannesburg, Eldorado, Magic, and McGregor) and hanging glaciers; some days, you may be able to hear the roar of ice calving from the glaciers on Johannesburg Mountain. Wildflowers—including yellow glacier lilies and pink-blossomed mountain heather—abound after snowmelt, providing a bright counterpoint to the greens, blacks, and whites of their environs. The trail has been popular for countless generations; Native Americans followed the Cascade Pass to reach the eastern side of the mountains, and gold and silver prospectors also followed the route. (There are remnants of a mining site at nearby Horseshoe Basin.)

"Most hikers stop at the pass," Michael continued, "but I like to make it an overnight trip by continuing on up Sahale Arm (another more rigorous two and a half miles, due north from the pass). Up the arm, right at the toe of Sahale Glacier, there's a designated camping site—the highest in the park. From here, you have panoramic views of a sea of tightly packed needles and pinnacles and glaciers that seem to extend forever, rolling down in waves behind you. When you're up high enough in the North Cascades, you can see the big volcanoes—Baker, Glacier Peak, sometimes even Mount Rainier, which is south of Seattle. This vertical topography, combined with the snow and glaciers, makes up an iconic landscape that you don't see anywhere else in North America outside of Alaska. It's a scene very endemic to the Pacific Northwest."

One of Michael's fondest memories of the North Cascades concerns his first ascent of ice-clad Mount Baker, the highest point in the North Cascades at 10,778 feet. "My wife and I had begun spending time in the Pacific Northwest, and we took a weekend to climb Mount Baker at the northwest section of the region. It was late morning, and we'd made it pretty far up the mountain, but the weather had been bad. As heavy fog enveloped us and the wind came up, we decided to set up our tent and wait it out. After trying to warm up for a while, we realized that the tent wasn't rattling anymore. We poked our heads out. Not only had the winds calmed down, but the clouds had dropped below us. We were staring out at an ocean of pillowy, bright clouds, with just Mount Rainier and Mount Adams in sight to the south. We grabbed our gear and made our way up to the summit. When we reached it, we were alone—an uncommon experience, as this is a mountain that does get climbed with some frequency. It was the first of the major Pacific Northwest peaks that I'd climbed.

"Thinking back on that experience, I look forward to the time when my kids will have the stamina to climb Mount Baker and hike the trails of the North Cascades."

MICHAEL LANZA is a freelance writer and photographer, and is Northwest editor of *Backpacker* magazine. He has covered topics as diverse as the controversy over snowmobiles in Yellowstone and the impact of climate change on Glacier National Park and other wild lands; his articles about global warming helped *Backpacker* earn a National Magazine Award for general excellence in 2008. He has published stories in several magazines about adventure travels on four continents. He's the author of several books, including *Seven Summits: The High Peaks of the Pacific Northwest, Winter Hiking and Camping, Day Hiker's Handbook, New England Hiking,* and *The Ultimate Guide to Backcountry Travel.* Michael's experience includes syndicating a weekly outdoors column in twenty daily newspapers across New England, editing an outdoors magazine, cohosting a call-in show about the outdoors on New Hampshire Public Radio, and working as a reporter and editor at Massachusetts and New Hampshire newspapers. An avid backpacker, climber, backcountry skier, and cyclist, he has hiked and climbed extensively in the U.S. West and Northeast, and in the Alps, Canadian Rockies, Himalaya, Iceland, Patagonia, New Zealand's Southern Alps, Spain, and the Scottish Highlands. Michael lives in Boise, Idaho, with his wife, Penny Beach, and their son, Nate, and daughter, Alex.

If You Go

▶ **Getting There:** The western entry point to North Cascades National Park is roughly three hours from Seattle and Vancouver, which are both served by many major carriers.

▶ **Best Time to Visit:** The park is open year-round, though hiking trails are most likely to be clear of snow (and the weather the driest) from mid-June to September. The North Cascades National Park Web site (www.nps.gov/noca) provides abundant trail and back-country information.

▶ **Accommodations:** The town of Marblemount is near the western entrance of the park; lodging options here are highlighted at the North Cascades Visitor Information Center (360-873-4150; www.marblemount.com).

GRAND TETON NATIONAL PARK

RECOMMENDED BY **Rob Hess**

"Anyone who has driven through Jackson Hole and looked to the west at Grand Teton can't help but wonder, 'What would it be like to be on top of that thing?'" Rob Hess began. "Most don't have an opportunity, but a few do make it."

The Grand Tetons, just north of Jackson, Wyoming, are not America's tallest mountains, though they may be its most recognizable. Rising abruptly from the valley floor, the distinctive jagged peaks of the compact Teton Range are iconic of the American West and the national park that bears its name. Grand Teton National Park encompasses 485 square miles, making up the southern sector of the Greater Yellowstone ecosystem. Forested hillsides drop down to the banks of the shimmering Snake River, which runs north to south through the park. Beyond the river, the long valley unfolds. (The "hole" in Jackson Hole, Wyoming, incidentally, refers to the fifty-five-mile-long, thirteen-mile-wide valley, not the money pit that a vacation home in this highly desirable area represents.) There are 238 miles of hiking trails in the park, ranging from gentle walks around Jenny Lake to the ambitious backcountry Teton Crest Trail. And Grand Teton looms over it all.

There are twelve peaks in the Teton range standing more than 12,000 feet high that climbers can ascend—the big dog here, however, is Grand Teton itself, which measures 13,770 feet at its summit and rises some 7,000 feet from the valley floor. "Grand Teton is a very imposing mountain," Rob continued. "When people who have signed up to do the climb look at it, their first comment is often, 'There's no way I'll ever make it!' While the climb has some very technical elements, they're fairly finite; you're only on technical terrain a short period of time. Many people who show up have never touched a rope, and a few aren't necessarily in the very best of shape. Being in good cardiovascular condition is important, but you can have the most fit person imaginable out there, and if they don't

have the will, they won't be able to do it. I've seen people who aren't as fit as they should be make the climb, simply because they were able to keep at it."

For inexperienced climbers, Rob suggests a four-day program that gets people to the top of the mountain—and hopefully imparts some climbing skills as well. "We don't expect our new climbers to have the technical skills hard-wired after a day of training," Rob added. "We just want them ready to react when we have to perform a certain technique." The program unfolds like this: climbers get fitted with helmets and harnesses, then head off to the Lupine Meadows trailhead to begin the hike up to Jackson Hole Mountain Guides' Corbet High Camp, which rests at an elevation of nearly 11,000 feet. The hike to Corbet is a great initial test of your endurance, as you gain more than 4,000 feet over six hours. (The camp is well provisioned with tents, a kitchen, and requisite climbing gear, lightening your load a bit.) The first three hours to Lupine Meadows are fairly mellow; after lunch, switchbacks lead up the North Fork of Garnet Canyon. Corbet rests just below the east face of Grand Teton and the Teepe Glacier. "Beyond boasting spectacular scenery, the camp is extremely private," Rob continued. "We're also at the entrance to a cirque that provides great rock-climbing training."

On day two, the focus is on getting everyone comfortable with the technical aspects of rock climbing. "To make it to the top of Grand Teton, climbers need to execute three feats—technical scrambling, pitched climbing, and one rappel," Rob explained. "We walk through these techniques on nearby Garnet Towers. Participants learn by doing. Each technique is first demonstrated and then practiced." Climbers learn and review: knots, harnesses, and helmets; belaying, rappelling, and multipitch climbing systems; movement over rock, efficient ascent and descend methods. Preparations include at least one multipitch climb and rappel (often on a formation called All Along the Watchtower). In addition to practicing climbs and rappels, climbers have a chance to get acclimatized to the altitude, and build a rapport with and confidence in their guides.

"After dinner on day two, we brief people on the program for summit day," Rob continued. "We give people a sense of roughly when we're going to wake up, but don't tell them exactly when. If they know when they're supposed to get up, they may spend all night looking at their watches instead of sleeping. We're usually up by three, have a good breakfast of oatmeal, egg sandwiches, or bagels and cream cheese, and then we're walking using our headlamps. We descend to the climber's trail and then begin gaining elevation. A fifty-foot fixed rope takes us to Lower Saddle. We're usually here by five or five-

OPPOSITE:
Millions of
visitors have
stared in wonder
at Grand Teton,
but few make it
to the top.

DESTINATION

49

thirty. From here, it's on toward Upper Saddle. At this point, there's some scrambling; it's not especially difficult, but the consequences of a fall are serious, so people are roped up. We're generally on Upper Saddle (13,000 feet) by seven or seven-thirty, and the air is warming with the sunlight. At this point, we don our stack ropes and tie in for the two or three pitched climbs we have ahead. The last 200 feet are an exposed, though fairly easy scramble. Between eight-thirty and ten-thirty, we're on the summit. On a clear day, you can view fourteen different mountain ranges in four states! You've covered 2,700 feet this morning, and a total of 7,000 since we started."

After some well-deserved celebration, it's time to head down. "We like to be off the summit before noon to hedge our bets against the weather—especially lightning," Rob explained. The exhilaration is not over yet, as your free rappel awaits. Climbers launch themselves out into space, hanging above the other peaks of the Tetons, buoyed not only by the ropes, but by their faith in their guides and themselves. "We're usually back in Corbet Camp by two or two-thirty," Rob added. "We have the option of hiking all the way out, though most people are content to relax in camp, have a nice dinner, and relish their accomplishment.

"We keep a logbook in the kitchen hut at Corbet where people who've made the climb can write their reflections, poems, or even drawings and pictures. The most common guest sentiment is, 'I didn't think I could do it, it seemed so big. Thanks for pushing me through.'"

ROB HESS is one of only several guides nationwide who is certified by the International Federation of Mountain Guide Associations (IFMGA), the foremost guide-certification organization worldwide. He was the third American to climb Mount Everest without oxygen. Rob has also successfully guided Broad Peak (26,440 feet) in Pakistan's Karakoram Range. He is the technical director of the American Mountain Guides Association, and in 2007 received their Outstanding Guide of the Year award. Rob is an owner of Jackson Hole Mountain Guides.

If You Go

▶ **Getting There:** Wyoming's Jackson Hole Airport is served by Delta (800-221-1212; www.delta.com) and United Airlines (800-864-8331; www.united.com). Some visitors will fly into Salt Lake City (served by most major carriers) and drive to Jackson, approximately six hours.

▶ **Best Time to Visit:** Guided climbs of Grand Teton are led from June through mid-September. Climbs are weather-dependent. Visit www.nps.gov/grte regarding other hiking opportunities in Grand Teton National Park.

▶ **Accommodations:** Lodging options and campgrounds are available in Grand Teton National Park (307-739-3300; www.nps.gov/grte). The Jackson Hole Chamber of Commerce (307-733-3316; www.jacksonholechamber.com) lists lodging options in town.

▶ **Guides/Outfitters:** Several outfitters lead climbs of Grand Teton, including Jackson Hole Mountain Guides (800-239-7642; www.jhmg.com).

DESTINATION

49

THE WIND RIVER RANGE

RECOMMENDED BY **Roger Grissette**

"My first hike in the Wind River Range was also my first backcountry trip," Roger Grissette recalled. "A friend in Chicago approached me and said he was going on a backpacking trip to Wyoming, and that I might enjoy it. I had some trepidation about whether or not I could pull it off, given the altitude and the elevation gains involved, but then I looked at my friend's physique and thought, 'If he can do it, I certainly can.' I made the trip and survived, and soon after I was leading trips in the Winds. More than twenty years later, I still try to get back every summer.

"The Wind River Range is not as well known as some of the other ranges in the Rockies. It's out of the way and hard to get to—some of my favorite trailheads involve several hours on very rough dirt roads to be reached. The time and energy it takes to get to the trailheads adds to the overall mystique and allure of the place."

The Winds stretch for a hundred miles along the Continental Divide in southwestern Wyoming; its northern terminus is roughly fifty miles southwest of Jackson as the crow flies. Though overshadowed by the Grand Tetons to the north in terms of notoriety, the Winds are quite formidable—forty-eight summits reach more than 12,000 feet, eight eclipse 13,500 feet, and the eastern face of the Rockies here is home to a many large glaciers, seven of the ten largest in the Lower Forty-eight. One of the most distinctive features of the Winds is the number of alpine lakes dotted across the range—more than a thousand of varying sizes, some containing trout. Indeed, the Winds are renowned in the angling community for horse-pack trips that explore the fishing possibilities of its remote waters. "On almost any trail you take in the Winds, you'll have excellent access to water—lakes, ponds, laughing streams. On the west side of the Divide, there's a beautiful string of lakes, including Dad's Lake and Marm's Lake. The hikes between these lakes

OPPOSITE:
Many consider
the Cirque of
the Towers
the signature
formation of
Wyoming's
Wind River
Range.

DESTINATION

50

are relatively easy, and they both have good fishing, with spectacular mountains for a backdrop."

Perhaps the most sought-after destination in the Wind River Range—and one that's not terribly difficult to reach—is Cirque of the Towers, in the southern section of the range. The Cirque is a spellbinding semicircle of jagged granite spires that tower above four lakes. The peaks—including Shark's Nose, Warbonnet, Warrior One, Wolf's Head, Pingora, and the tallest, Lizard Head (12,842 feet)—have a magnetic attraction for technical rock climbers, and an equal appeal for photographers. "In the 1940s and 1950s, word began to leak out about these towers that circle in a 300-degree arc around a group of lakes in the backcountry north and east of the Big Sandy Opening," Roger said. "They were so remote, they weren't climbed until 1940. You can get in a few ways—from the north, by following the Green River. This is a longer route, but it takes you past Square Top, a striking monolith that rises more than 3,000 feet abruptly from the river. Coming in from the Big Sandy Opening in the south, it's less than ten miles. On this approach, you follow gurgling streams up to a place called Jackass Pass. It's a steep climb up the pass as you cross over the Continental Divide, but before you reach the top, the tips of the first peaks come into view—Warbonnet and Warrior—an inspiration to keep going. From the top of the pass, it's a steep descent to Lonesome Lake, the only lake of the four here that has fish.

"The lake is the headwaters of the Popo Agie River, which, I believe, means 'head waters' in the Shoshone language. Whenever I'm here, I'm put in mind of the Shoshone, whose reservation is to the east. Their religion held that if you lived a proper life, your soul would be brought to the peaks of the Cirque. It was the happy hunting ground, with plentiful water and plentiful game. When one of my fellow leaders or I take beginning hikers here, they look upon us as gods of sorts. They experience a sense of wonderment, a thrill that they're actually here looking at these awesome spires."

The Bridger Wilderness is still home to many of the Rockies' iconic mammals— moose, elk, bighorn sheep, black and grizzly bears, mountain lion, and, more recently, gray wolf—though you may come away thinking that the animals are on vacation. "Some of the people I've taken through the Winds are a little disappointed that we don't see a lot of larger fauna," Roger said. "The large animals hear and smell us from a ways off and make themselves scarce. Local rangers tell me that every trip you make into this backcountry, you have a bear encounter—except only the bear knows about it!"

Summers in the Wind River Range can offer up idyllic weather—warm, sunny days and crisp, cool nights. But in this high, exposed country, winter is never far away. "On a trip some years back, I was crossing into the Winds from the north, through a pass near Mount Hooker," Roger recalled. "It was spitting sleet and snow, and I was very uncomfortable. I remember looking down at my feet, and the ground was covered with thick mats of brightly colored alpine flowers. It didn't matter that it was snowing. In the Winds it's a short season, and flowers have to propagate while they can."

ROGER GRISSETTE is a frequent volunteer leader for Sierra Club Outings. He has led trips for many years in the Rocky Mountains of New Mexico, Colorado, Montana, Idaho, and Wyoming, as well as the Eastern Sierra Nevada, Utah, Mexico, and Hawaii. Leading four to five trips per year recently, Roger is thrilled to share these adventures and their sense of discovery with a diverse group of Sierra Club members. "Sometimes I feel I'm preparing a dinner party," he says. When not backpacking, Roger spends his spare time playing traditional music with friends in a string band.

If You Go

▶ **Getting There:** Pinedale, Wyoming, is the staging area for Wind River hikers. Jackson Hole is the nearest airport (seventy miles away), and is served by Delta (800-221-1212; www.delta.com) and United Airlines (800-864-8331; www.united.com). Many will fly into Salt Lake City and drive to Pinedale, approximately four and a half hours.
▶ **Best Time to Visit:** Conditions are most reliable from June through mid-September, though even at this time, snow can be a possibility in the high passes.
▶ **Accommodations:** The Big Sandy Lodge (307-382-6513; www.big-sandy-lodge.com) is near one of the trailheads that leads to Cirque of the Towers. The Sublette County Chamber of Commerce (307-367-2242; www.sublettechamber.com) lists lodging options around greater Pinedale.
▶ **Guides/Outfitters:** Sierra Club Outings (415-977-5522; www.sierraclub.org/outings) leads trips each summer to the Wind River Range.

DESTINATION

50

Published in 2010 by Stewart, Tabori & Chang
An imprint of ABRAMS

Text copyright © 2010 Chris Santella

Photograph credits: Pages 12, 88, 118, 200: © Shutterstock; pages 14 and 216: © Jimmy Chin;
page 16: © Eric Rorer; pages 22, 52, 60, 64, 84, 126, 192, and 196: © Corbis; page 24: © Brady Binstadt;
page 28: © Tony Fuentes for Sierra Club; page 38: © Mountain Kingdoms Ltd., UK; page 44: © Bob Wizk;
page 48: © Jiri Foltyn; page 70: © Oscar Calero; page 78: © Kuma; page 80: © Ron Dalhquist; page 96: © Bob
Thayer; page 100: © Andrea Pelletier; page 104: © Luiz Felipe Rivera - luznatura; page 110: © Samuel M. Beebe for
Ecotrust; page 114: © MichaelLanza.com; page 122: © Lucyna Koch; pages 126 and 130: © Ultimate Hikes; page
140: © David P. Lewis; page 148: © Steve Terrill; page 152: © KE Adventure; page 156: © Mariusz S. Jurglelewicz;
page 160: © Warwick Lister-Kaye; page 168: © Sander van der Wen; page 172: © Michael Renney; page 176:
© Callum MacNab; page 184: © Mike Norton; page 188: © Vassi Koutsaftis/archlight-pictures.com; page 206:
© Matt Goetz; page 210: © David Snyder for North Cascades National Park; page 220: © Barbara & Laura Davis

Library of Congress Cataloging-in-Publication Data
Santella, Chris.
Fifty places to hike before you die : outdoor experts share the
world's greatest destinations / Chris Santella.
p. cm.
ISBN 978-1-58479-853-8 (alk. paper)
1. Hiking—Guidebooks. 2. Walking—Guidebooks. I. Title.
GV199.5.S26 2010
796.5109—dc22
20100059

Editor: Jennifer Levesque
Designer: Anna Christian
Production Manager: Tina Cameron
Fifty Places series design by Paul G. Wagner

This book was composed in Interstate, Scala, and Village typefaces.

Printed and bound in China
10 9 8 7 6 5 4 3 2

Stewart, Tabori & Chang books are available at special discounts when purchased in quantity for premiums
and promotions as well as fundraising or educational use. Special editions can also be created to specification.
For details, contact specialsales@abramsbooks.com or the address below.

ABRAMS
THE ART OF BOOKS SINCE 1949

115 West 18th Street New York, NY 10011
www.abramsbooks.com